G. FENG

CHONGQING TRAVEL GUIDE

Chongqing Delights: Your Expert Travel Guide

Contents

1

Chapter 1

INTRODUCTION

About This Guide

Welcome to the Chongqing Travel Guide! Whether you're a first-time visitor or a returning traveler, this guide is your essential companion for exploring one of China's most vibrant and dynamic cities.

In this guide, we aim to provide you with comprehensive and up-to-date information to help you make the most of your Chongqing adventure. From the moment you arrive until the time you bid farewell, you'll discover the best of what this city has to offer.

Chongqing at a Glance

Nestled in the heart of southwestern China, Chongqing, often referred to as the "Mountain City," is a metropolis that offers a captivating blend of modernity and tradition. This sprawling municipality, known for its dramatic landscapes and rich cultural heritage, has become a sought-after destination for travelers from around the world.

Key Highlights:

- **Geographical Diversity:** Chongqing's unique topography is one of its defining features. The city is situated at the confluence of the Yangtze and Jialing Rivers, with towering hills and cliffs enveloping its urban core. This geography has given rise to its nickname as the "Mountain City" and provides stunning vistas and picturesque river views.
- **Historical Significance:** Chongqing has a storied past, serving as the wartime capital of China during World War II. The city played a crucial role in China's history and has numerous historical sites, museums, and memorials that reflect this era.
- **Culinary Capital:** Chongqing is celebrated for its fiery and flavorful cuisine, particularly its renowned hot pot dishes. The city's cuisine is a harmonious mix of Sichuan and local flavors, delivering a fiery punch to your taste buds.
- **Rich Culture:** Chongqing boasts a vibrant cultural scene, with local traditions, festivals, and performing arts that provide a glimpse into the area's heritage and values.
- **Economic Hub:** As one of China's major economic centers, Chongqing has experienced significant growth and develop-

ment in recent years. This blend of tradition and modernity creates an exciting atmosphere for both locals and visitors.

· **City of Bridges:** Chongqing is a city of bridges, with numerous impressive structures connecting its various districts and crossing the two rivers. These bridges are not only engineering marvels but also offer breathtaking views of the city's skyline.

· **Warm Hospitality:** The locals are known for their warmth and friendliness, making travelers feel welcome and at home.

Whether you're drawn to the urban buzz of a thriving metropolis or the tranquil beauty of natural landscapes, Chongqing offers a little bit of everything. From the bustling streets and neon lights of the city center to the serene countryside and historic sites, there's something here for every traveler. So, prepare to embark on a journey that will leave you with a deep appreciation for the rich tapestry of Chongqing's culture, history, and stunning scenery.

Planning Your Trip

Planning a trip to Chongqing is an exciting endeavor, and proper preparation can make your journey both smooth and memorable. In this section, we'll provide you with essential information to help you plan your visit to this captivating city.

1. When to Visit:

- Chongqing has a humid subtropical climate, with distinct seasons. Consider your preferences when choosing the best time to visit. Spring (March to May) and autumn (September to November) are generally the most pleasant seasons with mild temperatures and less rainfall. Summers (June to August) can be hot and humid, while winters (December to February) are relatively mild but can be overcast and rainy.

2. Duration of Your Stay:

- Determine the duration of your trip based on your interests and the attractions you wish to explore. A typical visit to Chongqing can last from a few days to a week, allowing you to experience the city's highlights and nearby destinations.

3. Budgeting:

- Create a travel budget that accounts for transportation, accommodation, food, activities, and shopping. Chongqing offers options for travelers on different budgets, so plan accordingly.

4. Travel Documents:

- Ensure that your passport is valid for at least six months beyond your planned departure date. Check the visa requirements for your nationality, as they may vary. Apply for a Chinese visa well in advance, if necessary.

5. Language:

- While Mandarin is the official language, Chongqing's locals may also speak various dialects. Learning a few basic Mandarin phrases can be helpful, as English may not be widely spoken.

6. Health and Safety:

- Consult your doctor about any necessary vaccinations or health precautions before traveling. Be aware of potential health risks and safety concerns and follow recommended guidelines.

7. Currency and Banking:

- The currency used in Chongqing is the Chinese Yuan (CNY). Credit cards are widely accepted in major establishments, but it's a good idea to carry some cash for smaller transactions.

8. Communication:

- Make sure you have a working mobile phone and consider purchasing a local SIM card or international data plan for easy communication.

9. Packing Essentials:

- Pack suitable clothing for the season, comfortable walking shoes, a universal power adapter, and any specific items you'll need for your planned activities.

10. Research and Itinerary Planning:

· Research the attractions and experiences you wish to enjoy in Chongqing. Create a flexible itinerary to make the most of your time while allowing room for unexpected discoveries.

By addressing these key aspects of your trip planning, you'll be well-prepared to embark on a remarkable journey through Chongqing, ensuring a memorable and enjoyable visit to this vibrant city.

Tips for Travelers

As you prepare for your adventure in Chongqing, it's essential to be well-informed and prepared. These travel tips will help you make the most of your trip and ensure a smooth and enjoyable experience in this dynamic city.

1. Learn Basic Mandarin Phrases:

· While English is not widely spoken, knowing a few basic Mandarin phrases can go a long way. Learn common greetings, numbers, and essential travel phrases to facilitate communication.

2. Dress Comfortably and Respectfully:

· Chongqing's weather can vary, so pack appropriately. Ensure you have comfortable walking shoes and dress modestly when visiting temples and other religious or cultural sites.

3. Embrace Local Cuisine:

- Don't miss the opportunity to savor Chongqing's renowned cuisine. Try the hot pot, spicy Sichuan dishes, and street food. Be prepared for the spicy flavors, but don't hesitate to ask for milder versions if you're not a fan of extreme heat.

4. Stay Hydrated:

- The weather can get hot and humid, especially in the summer. Carry a reusable water bottle and stay hydrated throughout the day.

5. Stay Informed:

- Keep up with the latest travel advisories and local news. Familiarize yourself with Chongqing's neighborhoods and attractions before you arrive.

6. Respect Local Customs and Etiquette:

- Be aware of local customs, such as removing your shoes when entering someone's home and respecting elders. Public displays of affection should be avoided, as they may be considered impolite.

7. Bargain Politely:

- Bargaining is common in local markets and some shops.

However, be polite and respectful during negotiations. It's all part of the shopping experience.

8. Carry Cash:

- While credit cards are widely accepted in major establishments, it's a good idea to carry some cash for small transactions and in more local settings.

9. Be Cautious with Street Food:

- Chongqing's street food is delicious, but exercise caution. Choose vendors with clean and well-maintained stalls to reduce the risk of foodborne illnesses.

10. Stay Safe:

- Chongqing is generally a safe city, but it's wise to take standard precautions. Keep an eye on your belongings in crowded areas and be mindful of your surroundings, especially at night.

1 Prepare for the Weather:

- Check the weather forecast for your travel dates and pack accordingly. Be ready for sudden rain showers by carrying an umbrella or a lightweight rain jacket.

12. Respect the Environment:

- Chongqing's natural beauty is a treasure. Help preserve it by disposing of waste responsibly and respecting local wildlife.

These tips will not only enhance your travel experience but also help you navigate Chongqing with respect for its culture and environment. By being informed and prepared, you'll be well-equipped to enjoy all that this dynamic city has to offer.

2

Chapter 2

GETTING TO KNOW CHONGQING

Chongqing Overview

C hongqing, often referred to as the "Mountain City," is a metropolis located in the southwestern part of China. As one of the country's four direct-controlled municipalities, it holds a unique status, allowing it to function as both a city and a province, granting it significant political and economic influence. Chongqing's distinctive geographical and cultural features make it a captivating destination for travelers from around the world.

Geography and Topography:

- Chongqing is known for its dramatic geography. Nestled at the confluence of the Yangtze and Jialing Rivers, the city is characterized by hilly terrain, steep cliffs, and stunning river gorges. These geographical features have earned Chongqing the moniker "Mountain City."

History and Culture:

· Chongqing's history is rich and diverse. During World War II, it served as the wartime capital of China, hosting the government as it resisted Japanese occupation. The city played a vital role in China's history, and numerous historical sites and museums pay tribute to this era.

Economic Significance:

· Chongqing has experienced rapid economic growth in recent years and is considered one of China's major economic hubs. Its strategic location on the Yangtze River and its proximity to the Sichuan Basin make it a center for trade and commerce.

Culinary Capital:

· Chongqing is renowned for its fiery and flavorful cuisine. Hot pot is a local specialty, offering an immersive dining experience featuring spicy broths, fresh ingredients, and a variety of dipping sauces. The city's culinary scene showcases a harmonious blend of Sichuan and local flavors.

Urban and Natural Beauty:

· The city's urban areas are teeming with life, including modern skyscrapers, bustling markets, and vibrant neigh borhoods. However, Chongqing's natural beauty is equally captivating, with lush greenery, tranquil parks, and breathtaking river views.

Tourist Attractions:

· Chongqing is home to a multitude of attractions, including the Three Gorges Dam, Dazu Rock Carvings, Eling Park, and the Chongqing Zoo and Aquarium. These sites offer visitors the chance to explore a range of historical, cultural, and natural wonders.

Transportation Hub:

· With a well-connected transportation network, Chongqing is accessible by air, train, and bus. It also serves as a significant river port along the Yangtze River, further enhancing its role as a transportation hub.

Warm Hospitality:

· The people of Chongqing are known for their warmth and hospitality, making travelers feel welcome and at home. The city's culture emphasizes strong community ties and traditional values.

Modern and Traditional Harmony:

· Chongqing's unique charm lies in its ability to seamlessly blend modernity with tradition. The city's contemporary infrastructure, diverse entertainment options, and cultural heritage create a dynamic atmosphere that caters to a wide range of interests.

As you delve into the heart of Chongqing, you'll discover a destination that beautifully marries the old and the new, the urban and the natural, and the rich history with a promising future. Prepare to immerse yourself in this captivating city and explore the many facets of its culture, cuisine, and breathtaking landscapes. Whether you're a history enthusiast, a food lover, or an adventurer, Chongqing has something special to offer every traveler.

A Brief History

Chongqing's history is a tapestry of dramatic events and enduring resilience. The city's roots can be traced back over 3,000 years, to the time of the Ba and Shu cultures, which once thrived in the region. Over centuries, it transformed into a strategic trading and military hub.

During the Second Sino-Japanese War (1937-1945), Chongqing played a pivotal role as the wartime capital of China. The city served as a sanctuary for the Chinese government as it resisted Japanese occupation. The "Chongqing Spirit" emerged during this time, symbolizing the Chinese people's unwavering determination and resilience in the face of adversity.

In 1997, Chongqing's status was elevated to that of a direct-controlled municipality, signaling a new era of economic development and growth. The city has since evolved into a vital economic and transportation hub, thriving along the Yangtze River and the Sichuan Basin.

Chongqing's geographical features, characterized by steep hills, dramatic cliffs, and the confluence of the Yangtze and Jialing Rivers, have earned it the nickname "Mountain City." These natural elements not only define its breathtaking scenery but also challenge the city's urban planners to create innovative solutions for transportation and development.

Today, Chongqing stands as a vibrant symbol of modernity and tradition, where a rich historical legacy coexists with bustling markets, an eclectic culinary scene, and a dynamic urban landscape. The city's past as a wartime capital and its current role as an economic powerhouse come together to create a unique blend of culture and commerce, making Chongqing a destination that both honors its history and embraces the future.

Geography and Climate

Geography: Chongqing, often referred to as the "Mountain City," boasts a distinctive and breathtaking geography. Situated in the southwestern part of China, Chongqing's topography is characterized by dramatic hills, rugged terrain, and striking river gorges. This unique landscape has earned it the moniker "Mountain City."

Key Geographic Features:

- **Rivers:** Chongqing is located at the confluence of two major rivers, the Yangtze River (Chang Jiang) and the Jialing River. The meeting of these two waterways forms a stunning natural backdrop for the city.
- **Hills and Cliffs:** The city is enveloped by lush green hills and steep cliffs, creating a visually striking urban environment. Some neighborhoods are perched on the hillsides, offering panoramic views of the city and its rivers.
- **Three Gorges:** Chongqing serves as a gateway to the famous Three Gorges region, a natural wonder along the Yangtze River. This area includes the Qutang Gorge, Wu Gorge, and Xiling Gorge, each with its unique charm.

Climate: Chongqing experiences a humid subtropical climate characterized by distinct seasons. Here's a breakdown of its climatic features:

- **Spring (March to May):** Spring is one of the most pleasant times to visit, with mild temperatures and blooming flowers. It's ideal for outdoor exploration and sightseeing.
- **Summer (June to August):** Summers are hot and humid, with occasional heavy rainfall. Daytime temperatures can soar, making it important to stay hydrated and protect yourself from the sun.
- **Autumn (September to November):** Autumn is another delightful season, marked by cooler temperatures, lower humidity, and clear skies. It's an excellent time for outdoor activities and cultural exploration.
- **Winter (December to February):** Winters in Chongqing are relatively mild, but they can be overcast and rainy. While temperatures rarely drop below freezing, it's advisable to

bring layers and rain gear.

Rainfall: Chongqing receives ample rainfall, particularly during the summer months, which can lead to occasional flooding. The city's lush greenery owes much to its generous rainfall.

Geography and Climate's Influence: Chongqing's geography and climate have a significant impact on the city's character and daily life. The hilly terrain can pose transportation challenges, and the humidity during summer can be intense. However, these natural elements contribute to the city's stunning beauty and create a unique backdrop for the diverse urban and natural experiences it offers. Whether you're exploring the bustling city center or enjoying the tranquility of its parks and river vistas, Chongqing's geography and climate play an integral role in shaping the city's identity.

Culture and Traditions

Rich Tapestry of Culture: Chongqing, as a city with a long and diverse history, boasts a rich tapestry of culture that reflects the customs, traditions, and values of its people. Here are some key aspects of Chongqing's culture:

1. Diverse Ethnicity: While the majority of Chongqing's population is Han Chinese, the city is also home to various ethnic minority groups, including the Tujia, Miao, and Bai. These ethnic groups have contributed to the city's cultural diversity, influencing its traditions, festivals, and local customs.

2. Festivals and Celebrations: Chongqing celebrates a wide array of traditional Chinese festivals, such as Chinese New Year (Spring Festival), Mid-Autumn Festival, and Dragon Boat Festival. Local customs and celebrations add a unique flavor to these events. For instance, during the Spring Festival, residents of Chongqing participate in dragon and lion dances, as well as other traditional performances.

3. Chongqing Opera: Chongqing Opera, a traditional regional opera form, is a distinctive cultural treasure. It combines singing, acting, and acrobatics, often accompanied by a unique musical ensemble. The performances depict historical stories, folk tales, and local legends, offering a glimpse into the city's cultural heritage.

4. Local Dialects: Chongqing is known for its distinctive local dialect, often referred to as Chongqinghua or Sichuanese Mandarin. While Mandarin is the official language, many locals still converse in the Chongqing dialect, which holds a special place in the city's cultural identity.

5. Traditional Arts and Crafts: The city is known for its traditional arts and crafts, including Sichuan embroidery, porcelain, and bamboo weaving. These crafts have been passed down through generations and continue to be cherished by both locals and visitors.

6. Calligraphy and Painting: Chongqing has a strong tradition of calligraphy and painting, with many local artists and art schools dedicated to preserving and promoting these fine arts. You can often find art exhibitions and workshops throughout the city.

7. Tea Culture: Chongqing has a thriving tea culture, and teahouses are an integral part of daily life. Locals gather in teahouses to socialize, play games, and enjoy various types of tea. It's a great way to immerse yourself in the local culture and interact with Chongqing's residents.

8. Taoist and Buddhist Influences: Chongqing is home to numerous temples and monasteries, reflecting its historical ties to Taoism and Buddhism. The Dazu Rock Carvings, a UNESCO World Heritage Site near Chongqing, feature thousands of intricate Buddhist statues and carvings.

9. Respect for Elders: In Chongqing's culture, respect for elders is highly emphasized. It's common to address seniors with honorific titles and show deference in family and social interactions.

Chongqing's culture is a captivating blend of traditional Chinese customs, regional diversity, and modern influences. Whether you're enjoying the local cuisine, witnessing traditional performances, or participating in cultural festivals, you'll have the opportunity to explore and appreciate the unique cultural landscape that defines Chongqing.

Language and Communication

Mandarin as the Official Language: Mandarin Chinese is the official language of Chongqing and is widely used in government, education, and business. If you're familiar with standard Mandarin, you'll find it useful for communication in Chongqing.

Local Dialect – Chongqinghua: Chongqinghua, the local dialect, is distinct and widely spoken among locals. It's a variant of Sichuanese Mandarin, featuring unique vocabulary and pronunciation. While not necessary for basic communication, learning a few local phrases can enhance your experience and be appreciated by residents.

Common Mandarin Phrases: Here are some useful Mandarin phrases for travelers:

- **Hello:** (Nǐ hǎo)
- **Thank you:** (Xièxiè)
- **Yes:** (Shì de)
- **No:** (Bù)
- **Please:** (Qǐng)
- **Excuse me / Sorry:** (Duìbuqǐ)
- **I don't understand:** (Wǒ bù míngbai)
- **How much is this?:** (Zhège duōshǎo qián?)
- **Where is...?:** ... (...zài nǎlǐ?)
- **Restroom:** (Cèsuǒ)
- **Help:** (Bāngzhù)

English Proficiency: While Mandarin is prevalent, English proficiency can vary. In more tourist-oriented areas, you may find some level of English spoken in hotels, restaurants, and shops. However, it's advisable to have essential phrases and a translation app on hand, as English may not be widely spoken in local neighborhoods.

Translation Apps: Consider using translation apps or carrying a pocket dictionary to aid in communication, especially if you plan to explore areas less frequented by tourists.

Non-Verbal Communication: Non-verbal cues, such as pointing, gesturing, and using body language, can be effective means of communication when language barriers exist. Locals are often patient and willing to help when you make an effort to connect.

Respect and Politeness: Politeness and respect are valued in Chongqing's culture. When interacting with locals, using polite language and gestures is appreciated.

Cultural Sensitivity: Be mindful of cultural sensitivities, such as addressing people by their titles and avoiding public displays of affection, which may be considered impolite in Chinese culture.

Local Hospitality: Chongqing residents are known for their warmth and hospitality. If you show respect for the local culture and make an effort to communicate, you'll likely be met with friendliness and helpfulness during your visit.

In Chongqing, language and communication may present some challenges, but with a basic understanding of Mandarin and an appreciation for the local dialect and culture, you can navigate the city effectively and engage with its warm and welcoming residents.

3

Chapter 3

GETTING THERE AND AROUND

Getting to Chongqing

C hongqing, as a major transportation hub in China, is
well-connected to domestic and international destinations. Here's a guide on how to get to Chongqing:

By Air:

· **Chongqing Jiangbei International Airport (CKG):** This
is the main gateway to the city, serving both domestic
and international flights. The airport is located about 20
kilometers from the city center. It offers numerous daily
flights from major Chinese cities like Beijing, Shanghai, and
Guangzhou, as well as international routes.

By Train:

- **Chongqing Railway Station:** The city has several train stations, with Chongqing Railway Station being one of the main transportation hubs. High-speed trains connect Chongqing to cities like Chengdu, Xi'an, Wuhan, and Beijing. There's also the Chongqing North Railway Station, serving high-speed routes to destinations in northern China.

By Bus:

- **Long-Distance Buses:** Chongqing has a well-developed long-distance bus network that connects it to neighboring provinces and cities. You can take long-distance buses from various bus stations in the city, including Chongqing Bus Terminal and Chongqing Chenjiaping Bus Station.

By River:

- **Cruise Ships:** The city is a major river port along the Yangtze River. You can arrive in Chongqing via cruise ships, especially if you're taking a Yangtze River cruise. The Chaotianmen Port serves as the primary docking point for these cruises.

By Car:

- **Self-Driving:** If you're traveling from nearby cities, you can consider self-driving. Chongqing is connected to the national highway network, making road trips an option. Ensure you have the necessary permits and documents for driving in China.

Visa and Documentation:

- Ensure you have the appropriate travel documents, including a valid passport and visa, if required. Check the latest visa regulations and apply in advance if necessary.

Local Transportation:

Getting around Chongqing is relatively easy, thanks to a comprehensive public transportation system. This includes:

- **Metro:** Chongqing has a growing metro network with multiple lines that cover the city and its suburbs.
- **Buses:** Public buses are a cost-effective way to explore the city, with routes extending to various neighborhoods and attractions.
- **Taxis:** Taxis are readily available, but it's a good idea to have your destination written in Chinese or use a translation app to communicate with the driver.
- **Ride-Sharing:** Apps like Didi (the Chinese equivalent of Uber) are widely used for convenient transportation.

Language Consideration:

English may not be widely spoken, so it's helpful to have important addresses written in Chinese or use translation apps to aid in communication. Familiarize yourself with common Mandarin phrases for basic communication.

Getting to Chongqing is relatively straightforward, with multiple transportation options to suit your preferences and travel plans. Whether you're arriving by air, train, bus, or cruise ship, the city welcomes travelers with its unique blend of modernity and tradition, ready for exploration.

By Air

Chongqing is accessible from both domestic and international locations through Chongqing Jiangbei International Airport (CKG), which is one of the busiest airports in China. Here's how to get to Chongqing by air:

International Flights:

· If you are arriving from an international destination, check for flights to Chongqing Jiangbei International Airport. The airport handles international flights from major cities in Asia, Europe, and other parts of the world.

Domestic Flights:

· Chongqing is well-connected to major cities across China. There are frequent domestic flights from Beijing, Shanghai, Guangzhou, Chengdu, and many other cities. The airport serves as a crucial transportation hub, and you'll find numerous daily flights to Chongqing.

Getting to the City Center:

· Chongqing Jiangbei International Airport is located approx-imately 20 kilometers (12 miles) north of the city center.

There are several convenient ways to reach the city center from the airport:

- **Airport Shuttle:** The airport offers shuttle bus services that connect the airport to various locations in the city. This is a cost-effective and convenient way to get to your destination.
- **Taxi:** Taxis are readily available at the airport. Make sure to have your destination address written in Chinese or use a translation app to communicate with the driver. The journey to the city center by taxi takes around 30 to 40 minutes, depending on traffic.
- **Metro:** Chongqing's metro system has Line 10, which connects the airport to the city center. It's a convenient and affordable option, especially if you prefer public transportation.
- **Ride-Sharing Apps:** You can use ride-sharing apps like Didi to request a ride to your destination. These apps are widely used and can provide a convenient way to reach the city center.

Visa and Documentation:

- Ensure that you have your passport and any required travel documentation, including a valid visa if you're entering China. Check the latest visa requirements and ensure you have the necessary documents for your stay in Chongqing.

Chongqing Jiangbei International Airport is well-equipped to welcome travelers from around the world. Once you arrive in Chongqing, you'll find an array of transportation options and amenities to make your journey to the city center and your subsequent exploration of Chongqing convenient and enjoyable.

By Train

Chongqing is well-connected to other major cities in China through its extensive railway network. Traveling to Chongqing by train offers a scenic and comfortable option. Here's how to get to Chongqing by train:

High-Speed Trains:

- High-speed trains, known as "GaoTie" or "DongChe" in Chinese, are a popular and efficient way to reach Chongqing from various cities across China. Major high-speed train stations in Chongqing include Chongqing Railway Station and Chongqing North Railway Station.
- Here are some common high-speed train routes to Chongqing:
- From Chengdu: The journey from Chengdu to Chongqing is a popular high-speed rail route, taking around 1.5 to 2.5 hours, depending on the train type.
- From Xi'an: Trains from Xi'an to Chongqing take approximately 4 to 5 hours.
- From Wuhan: You can reach Chongqing from Wuhan in about 4 to 6 hours by high-speed train.

Conventional Trains:

- Conventional trains are also available, offering a more economical but slower travel option. Chongqing has train stations dedicated to conventional train services, including Chongqing Railway Station.

Getting to Chongqing Railway Stations:

- Chongqing Railway Station is centrally located in the city, offering convenient access to the urban core. Chongqing North Railway Station is situated in the northern part of the city.

Booking Tickets:

- Train tickets can be booked online through official websites, at train stations, or via authorized ticket agents. It's advisable to book your tickets in advance, especially during peak travel seasons.

Visa and Documentation:

- Ensure that you have your passport and any required travel documentation, including a valid visa if you're entering China. Verify the train station and its location in Chongqing to plan your arrival accordingly.

Traveling to Chongqing by train provides an opportunity to see the scenic beauty of the region and experience the efficiency and comfort of China's high-speed rail system. Once you arrive at the train station, you'll find various transportation options to continue your journey within Chongqing and explore its vibrant cityscape.

By Bus

Chongqing is accessible by long-distance buses from nearby cities and regions. Traveling by bus offers a cost-effective and adventurous way to reach the city. Here's how to get to Chongqing by bus:

Long-Distance Buses:

- Long-distance buses operate from various cities and regions, connecting Chongqing to neighboring provinces. These intercity buses offer a budget-friendly travel option.

Major Bus Stations:

- Chongqing has several major bus terminals, including:
- **Chongqing Bus Terminal (Chongqing Chongren Binguan Zongzhan):** Located in Yuzhong District, this terminal is one of the main bus stations in the city, serving routes to and from many destinations in China.
- **Chongqing Chenjiaping Bus Station:** Situated in Shapingba District, this station provides long-distance bus services to cities and regions in Sichuan and Chongqing.

Bus Routes:

- Buses operate from various cities and regions in southwestern China, including Chengdu, Guiyang, Xi'an, and more. There are regular bus services that cater to different preferences, such as standard coaches, sleeper buses, and express services.

Ticket Booking:

- Bus tickets can typically be purchased at the bus stations, online through official websites, or through authorized ticketing agents. It's advisable to book your tickets in advance, especially during peak travel periods.

Travel Duration:

- The travel duration by bus can vary significantly depending on the distance and route. For example, a bus journey from Chengdu to Chongqing may take around 3 to 4 hours, while longer journeys, such as from Guiyang, can take 6 to 8 hours or more.

Visa and Documentation:

- Ensure that you have your passport and any required travel documentation, including a valid visa if you're entering China. Verify the bus station and its location in Chongqing to plan your arrival.

Traveling to Chongqing by bus can be a budget-friendly and unique way to explore the scenic beauty of southwestern China. Upon arrival at the bus station, you'll find various transportation options to continue your journey within Chongqing and to its numerous attractions and neighborhoods.

Public Transportation and the Prices

Chongqing offers a comprehensive public transportation system that includes buses, the metro, and taxis. Here's an overview of public transportation in Chongqing, including typical prices:

1. Buses:

- Chongqing has an extensive bus network that covers the city and its suburbs. Buses are an economical way to get around. Fares typically range from ¥1 to ¥2 for non-air-conditioned buses and ¥2 to ¥4 for air-conditioned buses.

2. Metro:

- Chongqing's metro system is a convenient and efficient way to travel within the city. It has multiple lines that connect various neighborhoods and attractions. Metro fares are distance-based, with prices starting at ¥2 for short journeys. Longer journeys can cost up to ¥10 or more.

3. Taxis:

- Taxis are readily available in Chongqing and are a convenient way to get around, especially when you need to reach a specific location. The initial flag-down fare is typically around ¥8, and additional charges apply based on distance and time. Expect to pay more during peak hours.

4. Monorail:

- Chongqing also has a monorail system that operates in some areas of the city. It provides an alternative mode of public transportation.

5. BRT (Bus Rapid Transit):

- Chongqing's BRT system combines bus and metro-like features, providing efficient transport along designated corridors.

6. Smart Cards:

- It's advisable to purchase a transportation card for convenience and savings if you plan to use public transportation frequently. These cards can be loaded with credit and used for buses and the metro.

7. Ticketing:

- Bus and metro tickets can be purchased at stations, and you'll need to pay in cash or use your transportation card. When taking a taxi, fares are based on the taxi meter, and payment is made directly to the driver.

8. Note on Language:

- It's helpful to have destination addresses written in Chinese or use translation apps for communication, as English may not be widely spoken in public transportation settings.

Pricing and discounts may change over time, so it's advisable to check the most current fares and ticketing information when you arrive in Chongqing.

Public transportation in Chongqing is generally affordable and provides an excellent way to explore the city and its diverse neighborhoods, from the bustling city center to the scenic riverbanks and lush green parks. Whether you choose to travel by bus, metro, or taxi, you'll find that Chongqing's public transportation system is accessible and efficient.

Taxis and Ride-Sharing and Its Prices

Taxis and ride-sharing services are convenient options for getting around Chongqing, offering flexibility and accessibility. Here's an overview of taxi and ride-sharing services, including typical prices:

1. Taxis:

- Taxis in Chongqing are readily available and can be hailed on the street, at designated taxi stands, or through taxi-hailing apps. Chongqing taxis are generally yellow, and they have meters to calculate fares.
- **Initial Fare:** The initial flag-down fare for Chongqing taxis is typically around ¥8 to ¥10, depending on the time of day and the type of taxi.
- **Additional Charges:** Beyond the initial fare, additional charges are applied based on distance and time. These charges can vary, but they are typically around ¥2 to ¥3

per kilometer or ¥1 for every 2 minutes of waiting.

- **Peak Hours:** Fares during peak hours, such as rush hour, may be subject to a higher rate. For example, expect to pay more during morning and evening rush periods.
- **Extras:** If you need a larger taxi or have special requirements, such as carrying oversized luggage, there may be extra charges.

2. Ride-Sharing (e.g., Didi):

- Didi Chuxing is the most popular ride-sharing service in China and is widely used in Chongqing. You can use the Didi app to book rides with local drivers.
- **Pricing:** Ride-sharing prices are typically competitive with taxis. The app provides fare estimates, and you can choose from various vehicle options, including standard, express, and premium services.
- **Payment:** You can link your payment method to the app, making the payment process convenient and cashless.
- **Language:** The Didi app offers an English-language interface, making it accessible to international travelers.

3. Shared Rides:

- Both traditional taxis and ride-sharing services may offer shared rides in Chongqing, where you share the vehicle with other passengers heading in the same direction. This can reduce costs but may result in a slightly longer journey.

4. Price Fluctuations:

- Both taxis and ride-sharing services may have dynamic pricing during times of high demand, similar to surge pricing in other ride-sharing platforms. It's advisable to check the app for the most accurate pricing when booking a ride.

5. Accessibility:

- Ride-sharing apps are especially useful if you are unfamiliar with the local language, as they typically provide an English interface. Additionally, ride-sharing apps can be more reliable during peak hours, as you can book a ride in advance.

6. Payment Methods:

- Cash is accepted in taxis, but ride-sharing services like Didi typically require a linked payment method, such as a credit card or mobile payment app like WeChat Pay.

Prices for taxis and ride-sharing services can vary based on factors such as vehicle type, distance, and demand. While taxis offer the convenience of hailing a ride on the street, ride-sharing apps like Didi can provide a seamless and cashless experience. Be sure to check the app for the most up-to-date pricing when booking a ride in Chongqing.

Rental Cars/Prices

Renting a car can be an option for travelers who prefer more independence and flexibility in exploring Chongqing and its surrounding regions. Here's an overview of rental cars in Chongqing, including typical prices:

1. Car Rental Companies:

Chongqing has a number of international and local car rental companies that offer a variety of vehicles for rent. Major rental companies operating in Chongqing include Avis, Hertz, and local providers like eHi and Shenzhou.

2. Rental Costs:

- Rental costs can vary significantly depending on several factors, including the type of vehicle, rental duration, and the rental company. Here are approximate price ranges for car rentals in Chongqing:
- **Economy Car:** ¥200 to ¥300 per day
- **Intermediate Car:** ¥300 to ¥500 per day
- **SUV or Luxury Car:** ¥500 to ¥1,000 per day

3. Additional Costs:

- Be aware of additional costs such as fuel, insurance, and any optional services or accessories you may require. Fuel prices in China are relatively reasonable.

4. Driving License and Age Requirements:

- To rent a car in Chongqing, you'll typically need a valid international driving permit (IDP) or a Chinese driving license if you're staying in China for an extended period. Age requirements for renting a car vary by rental company but generally start at 21 or 25 years old.

5. Traffic Rules and Road Conditions:

- Familiarize yourself with Chinese traffic rules and regulations, and be prepared for driving in different traffic conditions and road styles. Chongqing's hilly terrain can present unique challenges, so exercise caution when navigating steep hills and narrow roads.

6. GPS and Navigation:

- It's advisable to have a GPS navigation system, whether it's included in your rental car or a portable device you bring with you. Navigation apps like Google Maps may not work reliably in China due to government restrictions.

7. Parking:

- Chongqing has parking facilities, but parking can be limited and may require fees in some areas. When exploring the city, it's essential to plan for parking, especially in the city center and popular tourist destinations.

8. Renting with a Driver:

- If you're uncomfortable with driving yourself or unfamiliar with local roads, consider renting a car with a driver. Many rental companies offer this service for a more stress-free experience.

Car rentals offer the freedom to explore Chongqing and its surroundings at your own pace. Before renting a car, be sure to research specific rental companies, their policies, and the driving conditions in the region. Prices and availability can vary, so it's a good idea to compare options and book in advance to secure the best rates and vehicle type for your travel needs.

Walking and Cycling

Exploring Chongqing by walking and cycling can be a rewarding way to experience the city's unique charm, especially in its hilly and scenic areas. Here's an overview of walking and cycling in Chongqing:

Walking:

1. **City Center Strolls:** Chongqing's city center, with its bustling streets and pedestrian-friendly areas, is perfect for leisurely walks. Explore the Jiefangbei Pedestrian Street, known for its shopping, dining, and vibrant atmosphere.
2. **Riverside Walks:** The confluence of the Yangtze and Jialing Rivers offers picturesque riverfront promenades. You can take a relaxed stroll along the riverside, enjoying stunning views of the city's skyline and the water.

3. **Parks and Green Spaces:** Chongqing has numerous parks and green spaces, such as Nanshan Botanical Garden and Eling Park, ideal for peaceful walks amidst natural beauty.

4. **Old Town Exploration:** Chongqing's older neighborhoods, like Ciqikou Ancient Town, provide an opportunity to explore charming alleys and historic architecture on foot.

5. **Hiking Trails:** For the more adventurous, Chongqing's hilly terrain provides ample opportunities for hiking. There are hiking trails that lead to scenic viewpoints and natural wonders.

Cycling:

1. **Shared Bikes:** Chongqing has a bike-sharing program, so you can easily rent bicycles for short trips. Look for bike-sharing stations throughout the city, unlock a bike using a smartphone app, and start pedaling.

2. **Cycling Routes:** The city offers designated cycling routes and bike lanes. Some areas along the riverside and in parks are particularly bike-friendly.

3. **Mountain Biking:** For mountain biking enthusiasts, the hilly terrain surrounding Chongqing provides a challenging and scenic environment for adventurous rides.

4. **Biking Tours:** Consider joining a guided biking tour if you want to explore the city and its surroundings on two wheels while learning about the local culture and history.

Safety and Tips:

· Be mindful of local traffic rules and exercise caution when cycling on busy streets.

- Always wear a helmet for safety, especially on challenging terrain.
- Use bike lights and reflective gear if cycling at night.
- Keep hydrated, wear sun protection, and carry essentials like water and a map.
- Respect pedestrians and fellow cyclists on shared paths.
- Consider the weather conditions, as Chongqing's summer can be hot and humid.

Walking and cycling provide a more intimate way to discover Chongqing's diverse neighborhoods, natural beauty, and local culture. Whether you choose to explore on foot or by bike, you'll have the chance to immerse yourself in the city's captivating sights and sounds while enjoying its unique topography and vibrant atmosphere.

4

Chapter 4

WHERE TO STAY

Chongqing Neighborhoods

C hongqing is a sprawling and diverse city with a wide range of neighborhoods to choose from. Here are some popular neighborhoods to consider, along with approximate price ranges for accommodations and nearby attractions:

1. Jiefangbei (Yuzhong District):

- *Price Range:* Mid-range to high-end options, with prices ranging from ¥300 to ¥800 per night for hotels.
- *Attractions:* Jiefangbei is the central business district of Chongqing, known for its shopping, dining, and nightlife. Visit the Jiefangbei Pedestrian Street for shopping and entertainment. Enjoy the vibrant cityscape and the iconic

People's Liberation Monument.

2. Guanyinqiao (Jiangbei District):

- *Price Range:* Mid-range to high-end options, with prices ranging from ¥250 to ¥700 per night for hotels.
- *Attractions:* Guanyinqiao is a modern commercial district with numerous shopping malls, restaurants, and entertainment options. It's a great place for shopping and experiencing contemporary city life.

3. Ciqikou (Shapingba District):

- *Price Range:* Budget to mid-range options, with prices ranging from ¥100 to ¥400 per night for hotels.
- *Attractions:* Ciqikou Ancient Town is a charming historic area with narrow alleyways, traditional architecture, and local street food. It's a cultural and culinary delight.

4. Hongyadong (Yuzhong District):

- *Price Range:* Mid-range to high-end options, with prices ranging from ¥300 to ¥700 per night for hotels.
- *Attractions:* Hongyadong is famous for its striking architecture built on the side of a hill, resembling traditional stilted buildings. It's a popular spot for shopping, dining, and enjoying Chongqing's unique urban scenery.

5. Nanbin Road (Yuzhong District):

- *Price Range:* Mid-range to high-end options, with prices

ranging from ¥300 to ¥800 per night for hotels.
· *Attractions:* This area along the Yangtze River offers stunning river views and a selection of high-end hotels and restaurants. Enjoy evening strolls along the riverbank and take in the city's modern skyline.

6. Shapingba (Shapingba District):

· *Price Range:* Budget to mid-range options, with prices ranging from ¥100 to ¥400 per night for hotels.
· *Attractions:* Shapingba is home to the Chongqing University and a thriving student culture. Explore local markets, street art, and the university campus.

7. Jiangjin (Jiangjin District):

· *Price Range:* Budget to mid-range options, with prices ranging from ¥100 to ¥500 per night for hotels.
· *Attractions:* Jiangjin is known for its beautiful rural landscapes, hot springs, and cultural sites. It's a great place to experience a more relaxed and countryside atmosphere.

8. Beibei (Beibei District):

· *Price Range:* Budget to mid-range options, with prices ranging from ¥100 to ¥400 per night for hotels.
· *Attractions:* Beibei is home to the Southwest University, and the area offers a mix of university culture, natural beauty, and local markets.

Prices for accommodations can vary depending on factors like location, hotel category, and seasonal demand. Chongqing's neighborhoods cater to a range of interests and budgets, ensuring that you can find the ideal place to stay while exploring the city's vibrant culture and attractions.

Budget Accommodations

Chongqing offers a variety of budget-friendly accommodation options for travelers. Here are some budget accommodations with approximate price ranges and nearby side attractions in the city:

1. Ciqikou Youth Hostel:

- *Price Range:* Typically around ¥100 to ¥250 per night for dormitories and private rooms.
- *Nearby Attractions:* Stay in the historic Ciqikou Ancient Town, famous for its traditional architecture, local street food, and cultural ambiance. Explore the narrow alleys and immerse yourself in the ancient atmosphere.

2. Bunk Youth Hostel:

- *Price Range:* Generally around ¥150 to ¥350 per night for dormitories and private rooms.
- *Nearby Attractions:* Located near Jiefangbei Pedestrian Street, you can easily explore Chongqing's central business district, shopping, and dining. Don't miss the People's Liberation Monument and scenic views of the Yangtze River.

3. Lazybones Hostel (Jiangbei Branch):

- *Price Range:* Typically around ¥100 to ¥300 per night for dormitories and private rooms.
- *Nearby Attractions:* This hostel is located in Jiangbei District, near Guanyinqiao, known for its modern shopping centers, restaurants, and entertainment options.

4. HI Chongqing Wulong:

- *Price Range:* Generally around ¥150 to ¥300 per night for dormitories and private rooms.
- *Nearby Attractions:* Located in Wulong County, this hostel provides access to the stunning Wulong Karst Landscape, a UNESCO World Heritage site. Explore the karst caves, natural bridges, and breathtaking scenery.

5. Hongyadong Youth Hostel:

- *Price Range:* Typically around ¥150 to ¥300 per night for dormitories and private rooms.
- *Nearby Attractions:* Stay in the heart of Hongyadong, an iconic part of Chongqing, and explore its stilted buildings, unique architecture, and vibrant street life.

6. Mr. Ka Hostel:

- *Price Range:* Generally around ¥100 to ¥250 per night for dormitories and private rooms.
- *Nearby Attractions:* Located in Shapingba, you can explore the local markets, street art, and the lively university cam-

pus of Chongqing University.

7. Garden Inn (Jiangjin Ancient Town):

- *Price Range:* Typically around ¥100 to ¥300 per night for private rooms.
- *Nearby Attractions:* Jiangjin Ancient Town offers a glimpse into traditional Chinese culture. Explore ancient architecture, temples, and local cuisine.

Please note that prices for budget accommodations may vary depending on the season, local events, and booking in advance. Staying in these budget-friendly places allows you to explore the city's diverse attractions while keeping your travel expenses in check.

Mid-Range Hotels

Chongqing offers a variety of mid-range hotels that provide a comfortable stay without breaking the bank. Here are some mid-range hotels with approximate price ranges and nearby side attractions:

1. Radisson Blu Plaza Hotel Chongqing:

- *Price Range:* Typically around ¥500 to ¥800 per night.
- *Nearby Attractions:* Located in the city center, this hotel is within walking distance of Jiefangbei Pedestrian Street, People's Liberation Monument, and various shopping and

dining options.

2. Hyatt Regency Chongqing:

- *Price Range:* Generally around ¥600 to ¥900 per night.
- *Nearby Attractions:* Situated in Yuzhong District, this hotel offers easy access to Hongyadong, where you can explore the unique stilted buildings, enjoy local cuisine, and take in the city's skyline.

3. Le Meridien Chongqing, Nan'an:

- *Price Range:* Typically around ¥550 to ¥800 per night.
- *Nearby Attractions:* This hotel in Nan'an District is conveniently located near Nanshan Botanical Garden, which offers beautiful natural landscapes and plant collections. It's also close to Yangtze River views.

4. Wanyou Conifer Hotel:

- *Price Range:* Generally around ¥400 to ¥700 per night.
- *Nearby Attractions:* Located near Guanyinqiao in Jiangbei District, this hotel provides easy access to shopping malls, restaurants, and modern entertainment.

5. Somerset Jiefangbei Chongqing:

- *Price Range:* Typically around ¥500 to ¥800 per night.
- *Nearby Attractions:* Situated in the central business district, this hotel is close to Jiefangbei Pedestrian Street, where you can enjoy shopping and dining. The People's Liberation

Monument is also nearby.

6. Holiday Inn Chongqing North:

- *Price Range:* Generally around ¥400 to ¥700 per night.
- *Nearby Attractions:* Located in Jiangbei District, this hotel provides access to Guanyinqiao, with its numerous shopping centers, dining options, and modern entertainment.

7. Niccolo Chongqing:

- *Price Range:* Typically around ¥600 to ¥1,000 per night.
- *Nearby Attractions:* This upscale hotel is in Yuzhong District, offering proximity to attractions like Jiefangbei Pedestrian Street, Hongyadong, and People's Liberation Monument.

Please note that prices for mid-range hotels can vary based on factors such as the time of year, availability, and room type. Staying in mid-range hotels in these central locations allows you to enjoy a comfortable stay while being close to some of Chongqing's most iconic attractions.

Luxury Hotels

Chongqing boasts several luxury hotels that offer upscale amenities and exceptional service. Here are some luxury hotels with approximate price ranges and nearby side attractions:

1. InterContinental Chongqing:

- *Price Range:* Typically around ¥800 to ¥1,500 per night.
- *Nearby Attractions:* Situated in Yuzhong District, the hotel is close to Jiefangbei Pedestrian Street, Hongyadong, and the People's Liberation Monument. Enjoy upscale shopping and dining in the city center.

2. Hilton Chongqing:

- *Price Range:* Generally around ¥700 to ¥1,200 per night.
- *Nearby Attractions:* Located in Yuzhong District, this hotel offers easy access to Jiefangbei, Hongyadong, and Nanshan Botanical Garden for leisurely strolls and natural beauty.

3. The Westin Chongqing Liberation Square:

- *Price Range:* Typically around ¥800 to ¥1,500 per night.
- *Nearby Attractions:* This hotel in Yuzhong District is within walking distance of People's Liberation Monument, Jiefangbei Pedestrian Street, and Hongyadong, allowing you to explore the vibrant city center.

4. JW Marriott Hotel Chongqing:

- *Price Range:* Generally around ¥800 to ¥1,400 per night.
- *Nearby Attractions:* Situated in Yuzhong District, this hotel is close to People's Liberation Monument, Jiefangbei Pedestrian Street, and the iconic stilted buildings of Hongyadong.

5. Niccolo Chongqing:

- *Price Range:* Typically around ¥1,000 to ¥2,000 per night.

- *Nearby Attractions:* Located in Yuzhong District, this luxury hotel offers easy access to Jiefangbei, Hongyadong, and People's Liberation Monument, making it ideal for high-end shopping and dining.

6. Kempinski Hotel Chongqing:

- *Price Range:* Generally around ¥700 to ¥1,400 per night.
- *Nearby Attractions:* This hotel in Yuzhong District provides access to Jiefangbei Pedestrian Street, Hongyadong, and Nanshan Botanical Garden for a mix of urban and natural attractions.

7. Banyan Tree Chongqing Beibei:

- *Price Range:* Typically around ¥900 to ¥1,800 per night.
- *Nearby Attractions:* Located in Beibei District, this resort-style hotel offers a tranquil escape, with access to the local culture, markets, and the Southwest University campus.

Please note that prices for luxury hotels can vary based on room types, seasonal demand, and special promotions. Staying in luxury hotels in Chongqing not only offers opulent accommodations but also grants you convenient access to some of the city's most iconic landmarks and vibrant neighborhoods.

Hostels and Guesthouses

Chongqing offers a variety of hostels and guesthouses, which are budget-friendly options for travelers seeking affordable accommodations. Here are some hostels and guesthouses with approximate price ranges and nearby side attractions:

1. Traveler's Youth Hostel:

- *Price Range:* Typically around ¥60 to ¥200 per night for dormitories and private rooms.
- *Nearby Attractions:* Located near the Ciqikou Ancient Town, you can explore the charming streets, traditional architecture, and local street food. The ancient town is known for its cultural and historical significance.

2. Chongqing Travelling With Hostel (Nanping Branch):

- *Price Range:* Generally around ¥80 to ¥250 per night for dormitories and private rooms.
- *Nearby Attractions:* This hostel is situated in Yuzhong District, close to Hongyadong, where you can explore stilted buildings, enjoy local cuisine, and take in the city's skyline.

3. Dekang Hostel:

- *Price Range:* Typically around ¥80 to ¥250 per night for dormitories and private rooms.
- *Nearby Attractions:* This hostel is located in Jiangbei District, providing access to Guanyinqiao's modern shopping centers, restaurants, and entertainment options.

4. Sim's Hostel:

- *Price Range:* Generally around ¥70 to ¥200 per night for dormitories and private rooms.
- *Nearby Attractions:* This hostel is in Shapingba District, known for its student culture, local markets, street art, and Chongqing University campus.

5. Bamboo International Youth Hostel:

- *Price Range:* Typically around ¥60 to ¥180 per night for dormitories and private rooms.
- *Nearby Attractions:* This hostel in Yuzhong District is within walking distance of the Jiefangbei Pedestrian Street, where you can explore shopping and dining options, along with the People's Liberation Monument.

6. Mad House Hostel:

- *Price Range:* Generally around ¥80 to ¥250 per night for dormitories and private rooms.
- *Nearby Attractions:* Located in Yuzhong District, this hostel provides easy access to Jiefangbei Pedestrian Street, Hongyadong, and People's Liberation Monument.

7. Shapingba Green Forest Hostel:

- *Price Range:* Typically around ¥60 to ¥180 per night for dormitories and private rooms.
- *Nearby Attractions:* Stay in Shapingba District to explore the local markets, street art, and Chongqing University campus,

which has a vibrant student culture.

Please note that prices for hostels and guesthouses can vary depending on factors like the time of year, availability, and room type. Staying in these budget-friendly accommodations allows you to explore Chongqing's attractions while keeping your travel costs in check.

Unique Accommodation Options

If you're looking for distinctive and unconventional places to stay in Chongqing, the city offers some unique accommodation options that provide memorable experiences. Here are a few unique accommodations with approximate price ranges and nearby side attractions:

1. Stilted Houses in Hongyadong:

- *Price Range:* Prices for stilted houses in Hongyadong can vary widely, but expect to pay around ¥500 to ¥1,500 per night.
- *Nearby Attractions:* Staying in a stilted house in Hongyadong offers an immersive experience itself. Explore the charming alleys, shops, and restaurants within this iconic riverside district. Enjoy breathtaking views of the city skyline and the confluence of the Yangtze and Jialing Rivers.

2. Karst Cave Hotels in Wulong:

- *Price Range:* Typically around ¥300 to ¥800 per night.
- *Nearby Attractions:* These unique hotels provide access to the stunning Wulong Karst Landscape, a UNESCO World Heritage site. Explore the karst caves, natural bridges, and picturesque countryside.

3. Treehouse Accommodations in the Countryside:

- *Price Range:* Generally around ¥200 to ¥600 per night.
- *Nearby Attractions:* Staying in a treehouse in the countryside offers a serene escape from the urban environment. Enjoy nature walks, local culture, and rural landscapes. Some treehouse accommodations are located in scenic areas like Jiangjin or surrounding counties.

4. Boutique Art Hotels:

- *Price Range:* Prices for boutique art hotels can vary widely but are generally around ¥500 to ¥1,500 per night.
- *Nearby Attractions:* Some boutique art hotels in Chongqing feature contemporary art installations, unique design, and immersive cultural experiences. Explore local and international art scenes, and enjoy the artistic ambiance of your hotel.

5. Riverside Boathouse Accommodations:

- *Price Range:* Typically around ¥200 to ¥600 per night.
- *Nearby Attractions:* Staying in a boathouse on the Yangtze River allows you to experience the river's unique culture and landscapes. Enjoy river views, riverside walks, and boat

rides.

6. Tea Plantation Stays:

- *Price Range:* Generally around ¥300 to ¥800 per night.
- *Nearby Attractions:* Accommodations in tea plantations, such as those in the nearby counties, provide a tranquil escape. Explore tea cultivation, traditional tea ceremonies, and the lush green scenery of tea fields.

Please note that prices for unique accommodations can vary based on factors like the time of year, room type, and special packages. Staying in these unique places allows you to not only enjoy distinctive accommodations but also explore the specific attractions and environments associated with each option.

5

Chapter 5

WHAT TO EAT IN CHONGQING

Chongqing Cuisine Overview

Chongqing is renowned for its unique and flavorful cuisine, which is characterized by spicy and bold flavors, often with a numbing sensation from Sichuan peppercorns. Here's an overview of some iconic dishes and the culinary highlights of Chongqing cuisine:

1. Hotpot ():

- Chongqing hotpot is legendary, and it's a must-try when visiting the city. The broth, typically divided into two sections – spicy and non-spicy, is brought to a boil at your table. You can then cook various ingredients, including thinly sliced meats, vegetables, mushrooms, and tofu, in the bubbling broth. The spicy version is famous for its use of chili peppers and Sichuan peppercorns.

2. Chongqing Spicy Chicken ():

· This dish features diced chicken chunks that are deep-fried until crispy and then stir-fried with a spicy sauce made with dried red chilies, garlic, and Sichuan peppercorns. It's known for its fiery flavor.

3. Mapo Tofu ():

· A classic Sichuan dish, Mapo Tofu features soft tofu cubes in a spicy and numbing sauce made with chili bean paste, minced pork, and Sichuan peppercorns. It's both spicy and savory, with a silky texture.

4. Chongqing Noodles ():

· Chongqing noodles are a beloved street food. They consist of thin wheat noodles in a spicy and flavorful broth. Toppings can include minced meat, peanuts, and fresh cilantro.

5. Dry-Fried Green Beans ():

· These green beans are stir-fried until they're blistered and slightly crispy, then tossed in a savory, spicy sauce. They're a popular vegetable dish.

6. Chongqing Liangfen ():

· Chongqing Liangfen is a cold dish made with jelly-like

rice or mung bean noodles, typically served with a spicy, vinegary sauce and various toppings like peanuts, chili oil, and green onions.

7. Chongqing Crispy Duck ():

- This dish features marinated duck that's been slow-cooked and then deep-fried to achieve a crispy exterior while retaining tender meat. It's served with a dipping sauce.

8. Suanla Fen ():

- Suanla Fen is a spicy and sour noodle soup that's beloved by locals. It features rice noodles in a tangy and spicy broth, often topped with minced meat, peanuts, and vegetables.

9. Chongqing Beer ():

- While not a dish, Chongqing has a thriving beer culture. Enjoy local Chongqing beer, which pairs well with the spicy cuisine, in many restaurants and bars.

Chongqing cuisine is known for its bold and fiery flavors, making it a paradise for lovers of spicy food. Many of these dishes incorporate chili peppers and Sichuan peppercorns, which create a complex combination of heat and numbing sensations. Don't miss the opportunity to explore the vibrant culinary scene and savor the diverse flavors of Chongqing when you visit.

Famous Dishes and Street Food

Chongqing is known for its vibrant street food culture, with an array of delicious and unique dishes. Here are some famous dishes and street foods you should definitely try when visiting the city:

1. Xiaomian ():

- Chongqing is famous for its spicy noodles, commonly known as xiaomian. These are often served in small eateries and street stalls, and you can choose the level of spiciness. The noodles are served in a flavorful and spicy broth, often garnished with minced meat, peanuts, and fresh herbs.

2. Chuan Chuan Xiang ():

- Chuan Chuan Xiang is a popular type of hotpot served on skewers. You pick the skewers with the ingredients you want, and they are cooked in a communal spicy broth. It's a favorite choice for locals and tourists alike.

3. Stinky Tofu ():

- This fermented tofu has a strong odor but a unique and delicious flavor. It's deep-fried and served with a spicy dipping sauce. Locals often enjoy it as a popular street food snack.

4. Grilled Skewers ():

- You'll find numerous street stalls offering grilled skewers with a variety of ingredients like meat, vegetables, and seafood. These skewers are seasoned with spices and often coated with chili sauce for a flavorful kick.

5. Fried Dumplings ():

- Chongqing-style fried dumplings are known for their crispy bottoms and juicy fillings. They are commonly filled with minced meat, vegetables, and seasonings.

6. BBQ Fish ():

- BBQ fish, often catfish, is prepared with a rich and spicy sauce. The dish is known for its deep flavors and is a Chongqing specialty.

7. Mala Tang ():

- Mala Tang is a type of spicy soup hotpot where you choose ingredients that are cooked in a spicy broth. It's customizable, allowing you to select your preferred combination of ingredients.

8. Duck Neck ():

- Duck neck is a popular snack often marinated in a spicy sauce. It's flavorful and addictive.

9. Wonton Noodles ():

- Chongqing's version of wonton noodles features succulent dumplings and thin noodles in a spicy and savory broth.

10. Glutinous Rice Cakes ():

- These are often stir-fried with vegetables, meat, and a spicy sauce, creating a unique and delightful texture and flavor.

When exploring Chongqing, be sure to visit local markets, food stalls, and small eateries to experience the full range of street food and famous dishes the city has to offer. Chongqing's street food scene is a sensory delight for food lovers.

Dining Etiquette

When dining in Chongqing or anywhere in China, it's important to be mindful of local dining etiquette to show respect for the culture and make your dining experience enjoyable. Here are some dining etiquette tips for Chongqing:

1. Seating Arrangement:

- In formal settings, there may be a seating arrangement based on hierarchy or age. Wait for the host to guide you to your seat. The most honored guest or eldest should be seated with their back to the wall or facing the entrance.

2. Table Manners:

- **Chopsticks:** Do not stick chopsticks upright in a bowl of rice, as this resembles a funeral ritual. Instead, place them on the chopstick rest or across your bowl.
- **Soup:** When eating soup, use your spoon or chopsticks to drink from the bowl. It's acceptable to slurp your noodles as a sign that you are enjoying the meal.
- **Spitting:** It's considered impolite to spit food out in public. If you need to remove an unpleasant piece of food from your mouth, discreetly use a tissue or napkin.

3. Sharing:

- Chinese meals are typically shared among all diners. Dishes are placed in the center of the table, and everyone takes from the communal plates. Use the serving utensils provided, not your own chopsticks, to take food from shared dishes.

4. Toasting (Ganbei):

- When making a toast, it's common to raise your glass and say "Ganbei," which means "bottoms up." If someone toasts you, it's customary to return the gesture.

5. Refusing Food:

- It's polite to try everything offered to you, even if it's just a small portion. If you don't want more of a particular dish, you can leave a small amount on your plate. If you're full, rest your chopsticks and decline politely.

6. Paying the Bill:

- In many Chinese cultures, there is often a friendly competition over who pays the bill. It's customary to offer to pay, but expect some resistance. Eventually, the person who invited everyone often pays.

7. Tipping:

- Tipping is not a common practice in China, including Chongqing. Instead, good service is appreciated but not usually rewarded with extra money. In upscale restaurants, a service charge may be included in the bill.

8. Leaving the Table:

- When you need to leave the table, place your chopsticks on your plate or in a chopstick holder. Leaving them sticking upright in a bowl is considered inauspicious.

9. Politeness and Gratitude:

- Express gratitude to the host and fellow diners, especially if someone has invited you. A simple "xie xie" (thank you) is appreciated.

By following these dining etiquette guidelines, you can show respect for Chongqing's cultural traditions and enjoy a more harmonious dining experience. Keep in mind that people in Chongqing are generally understanding of cultural differences, so if you make a mistake, they are likely to be forgiving and appreciative of your effort to embrace their customs.

Where to Eat

When it comes to dining in Chongqing, you have a wide range of options, from street food stalls to upscale restaurants. Here are some recommendations for where to eat in Chongqing:

1. Jiefangbei Pedestrian Street:

- Located in the city center, this bustling area is home to numerous restaurants, from traditional Chongqing hotpot to international cuisine. It's a great place to experience the local food scene.

2. Ciqikou Ancient Town:

- This historic district is not only a popular tourist spot but also a great place to savor Chongqing's traditional dishes. You'll find local street food stalls, teahouses, and small eateries.

3. Hongyadong:

- This iconic stilted building complex in Yuzhong District is known for its unique dining establishments. Enjoy dining with a view of the river and the city's skyline.

4. Guanyinqiao:

- Located in Jiangbei District, Guanyinqiao is a modern commercial district with numerous restaurants, cafes, and bars. It's a great place for international and local cuisine.

5. Shapingba District:

- The Shapingba area is known for its student culture and local cuisine. Explore the vibrant food scene around Chongqing University and other universities in the district.

6. Riverside Dining:

- Along the Yangtze and Jialing Rivers, you'll find restaurants and eateries offering both Chongqing specialties and international dishes. The riverside setting provides a lovely atmosphere for dining.

7. Local Street Stalls:

- Don't miss the opportunity to explore the street food culture in Chongqing. You'll find street vendors selling noodles, skewers, buns, and other local snacks all around the city.

8. Food Markets:

- Chongqing has several food markets where you can try a variety of local dishes. Popular options include Jiaochangkou Night Market and Nanbin Road Food Street.

9. Tea Houses:

- Chongqing has a rich tea culture, and you can enjoy tea at traditional teahouses. Many of these places also serve light snacks and meals.

10. Upscale Restaurants:

- If you're looking for a more upscale dining experience, you can find luxury restaurants in Chongqing, often located in high-end hotels. These restaurants offer both Chinese and international cuisine.

Whether you're in the mood for a fiery Chongqing hotpot, spicy Sichuan dishes, or international cuisine, Chongqing has dining options to suit all tastes and budgets. Be sure to explore the local food scene and savor the flavors of this vibrant city.

Local Eateries

Exploring local eateries is a fantastic way to experience the authentic flavors of Chongqing. Here are some local eateries and dining establishments you can consider:

1. Chongqing Hotpot Restaurants:

- Try the city's iconic hotpot at renowned local hotpot restaurants like Haidilao, Little Swan (Xiaoyang Shuan), and Qiu's Hotpot. These establishments offer a variety of broth options, meats, and condiments to customize your hotpot experience.

2. Xiaomian (Small Noodle) Shops:

- Local noodle shops specializing in xiaomian are scattered

throughout Chongqing. These small eateries offer spicy noodle dishes with various toppings and are perfect for a quick and flavorful meal.

3. Ciqikou Ancient Town Eateries:

· Explore the charming streets of Ciqikou and visit traditional teahouses and small restaurants. You can savor local specialties like stinky tofu, Chongqing noodles, and street snacks.

4. Local Sichuan Restaurants:

· Chongqing is part of the Sichuan region, so you'll find local Sichuan restaurants that serve fiery and flavorful dishes. These restaurants offer classic Sichuan dishes like Mapo Tofu, Kung Pao Chicken, and Yu Xiang Eggplant.

5. Street Food Stalls:

· Don't miss the opportunity to sample Chongqing's street food. Visit food stalls that line the streets and markets, where you can enjoy skewers, buns, fried dishes, and more.

6. Jiaochangkou Night Market:

· This bustling night market in Yuzhong District is a popular spot for locals and tourists alike. You can try a wide range of Chongqing street food here.

7. Jiangbei Guanyinqiao Food Street:

· This modern commercial district offers a diverse array of dining options. You'll find local and international cuisine, from hotpot to Western restaurants.

8. Shapingba Student Eateries:

· The Shapingba area is known for its student culture, and you'll find numerous small eateries that offer affordable and delicious meals.

9. Yubei District Food Markets:

· Yubei District has a reputation for having some of the best local food markets. Explore these markets to taste Chongqing's traditional cuisine.

10. Huguang Guild Hall (Huguang Huiguan):

· This historic restaurant in the Yuzhong District serves traditional Chongqing dishes in a beautifully restored Qing Dynasty-era building. It's a great place to experience the city's culinary heritage.

11. Jiangjin County Local Eateries:

· If you're willing to venture outside the city center, Jiangjin County offers local eateries serving authentic Chongqing dishes and countryside specialties.

Exploring Chongqing's local eateries and street food stalls will allow you to discover the rich and diverse culinary culture of the city. Don't be afraid to try new dishes and flavors to fully appreciate the local cuisine.

International Restaurants

Chongqing also offers a variety of international restaurants catering to diverse tastes. If you're looking for international cuisine while in the city, here are some options to consider:

1. Mediterranean and Italian:

- **Mediterranean Fusion:** This restaurant in Yuzhong District offers a fusion of Mediterranean and Western cuisine, with a beautiful riverside setting.

2. Japanese and Sushi:

- **Nishimura Restaurant:** Located in Yuzhong District, this Japanese restaurant is known for its sushi, sashimi, and teppanyaki.

3. Korean:

- **Hwa Hyun Korean Restaurant:** Savor authentic Korean dishes in Jiangbei District, including barbecue and bibim-bap.

4. Indian:

- **Namaste Indian Restaurant:** Located in Yuzhong District, this restaurant offers a variety of Indian curries, tandoori dishes, and biryanis.

5. Thai:

- **Chaba Thai Restaurant:** You can enjoy Thai cuisine, including curries, noodles, and seafood, at this restaurant in Jiangbei District.

6. Western and Fusion:

- **Scott's Family Steak House:** A popular choice for Western food, this restaurant in Yubei District specializes in steaks, burgers, and other international dishes.

7. Vietnamese:

- **Pho Vinh Vietnamese Restaurant:** Savor traditional Vietnamese pho, spring rolls, and other dishes in Yuzhong District.

8. Pizza and Italian:

- **Pizza Hut:** Several Pizza Hut branches can be found in Chongqing, offering a range of pizzas and pasta dishes.

9. Brazilian Churrascaria:

- **Brasay Vino Churrascaria:** Experience Brazilian barbecue and a variety of meat cuts in Yubei District.

10. International Buffet:

- **Kempinski Hotel Chongqing:** The hotel offers an international buffet with a wide selection of dishes from around the world.

11. Fast Food Chains:

- Various international fast food chains, such as McDonald's, KFC, and Burger King, can be found throughout Chongqing.

These international restaurants provide a diverse range of culinary experiences, allowing you to enjoy familiar dishes from around the world while in Chongqing. Whether you're in the mood for European, Asian, or other international flavors, you'll find options to suit your preferences.

Vegetarian and Dietary Restrictions

If you have dietary restrictions or prefer vegetarian options, Chongqing offers choices to accommodate your needs. Here are some tips for finding vegetarian and accommodating restaurants in the city:

1. Vegetarian Restaurants:

- Seek out vegetarian restaurants, often referred to as "" (sùshí) in Chinese. These places specialize in meat-free and plant-based dishes. Some popular vegetarian restaurants in Chongqing include "Xiang Yu Shan Shui Vegetarian Restaurant" and "Zhai Zi Xiang Vegetarian Restaurant."

2. Hotpot:

- Many Chongqing hotpot restaurants offer a "yuan yang hotpot" option, where one side of the pot contains a spicy broth, and the other is non-spicy or mild. You can enjoy a vegetarian hotpot experience by selecting vegetables, tofu, mushrooms, and other meat-free ingredients.

3. Buddhist Monastery Canteens:

- Some Buddhist monasteries in Chongqing operate canteens that serve vegetarian meals. These are great places to enjoy wholesome vegetarian dishes in a peaceful setting.

4. Customize Your Dish:

- When dining at non-vegetarian restaurants, you can often request vegetarian versions of popular dishes. Ask for dishes without meat or with tofu and a variety of vegetables.

5. Use Food Apps:

- Mobile apps like Dianping or Meituan can help you find vegetarian or vegan restaurants in Chongqing. These apps often provide user reviews and ratings, making it easier to locate suitable options.

6. Learn Basic Phrases:

- Knowing some basic Chinese phrases for dietary restrictions can be helpful. For example, "wúròu" means "no meat," and "sùshí" means "vegetarian." You can use these phrases to communicate your dietary preferences.

7. Local Markets:

- Chongqing's food markets often offer a variety of fresh fruits, vegetables, and ingredients that you can use to prepare your own vegetarian meals.

8. Check Ingredients:

- Be sure to inquire about the ingredients in the dishes you order. Some Chinese dishes may contain hidden animal products, so it's essential to communicate your dietary restrictions clearly.

While Chongqing is famous for its spicy cuisine, you can find vegetarian and accommodating options with some planning and communication. When in doubt, asking restaurant staff or locals for recommendations or assistance can be quite helpful.

Culinary Experiences

In Chongqing, you can immerse yourself in a variety of culinary experiences that will give you a deeper understanding of the city's rich food culture. Here are some culinary experiences to consider:

1. Chongqing Hotpot Feast:

- A visit to Chongqing wouldn't be complete without indulging in a hotpot feast. You can choose from a wide range of hotpot restaurants, from the upscale to local joints. Try both the spicy and non-spicy broths, and savor a variety of meats, vegetables, and dipping sauces.

2. Noodle-Making Class:

- Participate in a noodle-making class to learn how to make Chongqing's famous xiaomian (small noodles) or other regional noodle varieties. It's a hands-on experience that allows you to appreciate the art of noodle-making.

3. Food Market Tours:

- Join a guided tour of local food markets, such as Jiaochangkou Night Market or Nanbin Road Food Street. You'll have the chance to sample street food, fresh produce, and unique local snacks.

4. Sichuan and Chongqing Cooking Class:

- Enroll in a cooking class to learn how to prepare authentic Sichuan and Chongqing dishes. You'll gain valuable skills and insights into the spices and techniques used in the local cuisine.

5. Tea Ceremony Experience:

- Chongqing has a rich tea culture. Visit a traditional teahouse to enjoy a tea ceremony, taste a variety of Chinese teas, and learn about tea etiquette.

6. Stilted House Dining:

- Dine in one of Chongqing's iconic stilted houses in Hongyadong. These unique structures house restaurants and offer breathtaking views of the city and rivers. Enjoy local and international cuisine with a stunning backdrop.

7. Chongqing Food Festivals:

- If your visit coincides with one of Chongqing's food festivals, such as the Chongqing Hotpot Festival, be sure to attend. These festivals feature food stalls, culinary competitions, and cultural performances.

8. Culinary Tours:

- Join a guided culinary tour of Chongqing, which will take you to local eateries, food markets, and historic sites. This is an excellent way to explore the city's food scene with the guidance of a local expert.

9. Local Restaurant Hopping:

- Create your own food adventure by hopping from one local restaurant to another, sampling various Chongqing dishes along the way. Ask locals for recommendations to discover hidden gems.

10. Try Unique Chongqing Dishes:

- Seek out and taste unique Chongqing dishes, such as Chongqing crispy duck, Chongqing stinky tofu, or street food delicacies like "duck blood tofu" or "chuan chuan xiang" (skewers).

Exploring Chongqing's culinary scene is an adventure in itself. These culinary experiences will allow you to savor the flavors, aromas, and traditions of Chongqing's diverse food culture. Don't forget to engage with locals and immerse yourself in the city's vibrant food culture.

6

Chapter 6

EXPLORING CHONGQING'S ATTRACTIONS

Chongqing's Top Attractions

Chongqing, with its rich history, unique culture, and stunning landscapes, offers a wide range of attractions to explore. Here are some of the top attractions in Chongqing:

1. Three Gorges:

- Chongqing serves as a gateway to the famous Three Gorges on the Yangtze River. A cruise along the river takes you through breathtaking natural scenery, including the Qutang, Wuxia, and Xiling Gorges.

2. Ciqikou Ancient Town:

- This well-preserved ancient town on the Jialing River offers a glimpse into Chongqing's history. Explore its narrow, winding streets, traditional architecture, teahouses, and street food vendors.

3. Hongyadong Stilted Buildings:

- These iconic stilted buildings along the Yangtze River in Yuzhong District offer a blend of modern and traditional architecture. You can dine, shop, and enjoy stunning views of the city.

4. Chongqing Zoo and Pandas:

- The Chongqing Zoo is home to adorable giant pandas. It's a great place to learn about these rare animals and other wildlife.

5. Jiefangbei Pedestrian Street:

- Located in the city center, this bustling street is a hub for shopping, dining, and entertainment. Don't miss the People's Liberation Monument and the surrounding vibrant atmosphere.

6. Dazu Rock Carvings:

- A UNESCO World Heritage site, the Dazu Rock Carvings are intricate stone sculptures and carvings dating back over a thousand years, depicting Buddhist and Taoist themes.

7. Chongqing Chaotianmen Dock:

· This historic dock area is a starting point for Yangtze River cruises. You can also explore the nearby square and enjoy riverside views.

8. Chongqing Grand Theater:

· This stunning modern building is an architectural master-piece. Even if you don't attend a performance, the exterior and the surrounding area are worth a visit.

9. E'ling Park:

· E'ling Park is a beautiful and serene park on the banks of the Yangtze River. It features landscaped gardens, pavilions, and offers panoramic views of the city.

10. Chongqing Science and Technology Museum: - This interactive museum is a great place for family outings, featuring hands-on exhibits related to science and technology.

11. Gele Mountain National Forest Park: - Located on the outskirts of Chongqing, this park offers hiking and outdoor activities amid lush forests, and it's known for its scenic vistas.

12. Huguang Guild Hall: - This historic site in Yuzhong District provides a cultural experience, with traditional performances, tea ceremonies, and a glimpse into Chongqing's history.

13. Eling Park Cableway: - This cableway ride provides spectacular views of the Yangtze River, the cityscape, and E'ling Park.

14. Porcelain Port: - This cultural and creative district on the Jialing River features galleries, studios, shops, and a variety of art installations.

Chongqing's attractions offer a blend of natural beauty, cultural heritage, and modernity. Whether you're interested in history, cuisine, or natural landscapes, Chongqing has something to offer every traveler.

Three Gorges Dam

The Three Gorges Dam is one of the most significant engineering projects in the world and a key attraction in the Chongqing region. Here's an overview of the Three Gorges Dam:

1. Location:

- The Three Gorges Dam is situated on the Yangtze River in Sandouping, Yichang, Hubei Province. While it's not located within Chongqing's city limits, it's a popular destination for tourists visiting Chongqing, as the city often serves as the starting point for Yangtze River cruises that pass by the dam.

2. Purpose:

- The primary purposes of the Three Gorges Dam are flood control, hydroelectric power generation, and improving navigation along the Yangtze River. It's a multi-functional infrastructure project.

3. Dimensions:

- The dam is approximately 2.3 miles (3.7 kilometers) long and about 607 feet (185 meters) tall. It's one of the largest concrete structures in the world. The dam's reservoir, known as the Three Gorges Reservoir, extends over a vast area and has significantly altered the landscape of the region.

4. Hydroelectric Power:

- The dam has a total generating capacity of over 22,000 megawatts, making it one of the world's largest hydroelectric power stations. It provides a substantial portion of China's electricity.

5. Flood Control:

- The dam plays a crucial role in controlling flooding along the Yangtze River. It has helped mitigate the devastating impact of seasonal floods and is designed to reduce the frequency and severity of flood events downstream.

6. Environmental Impact:

- The construction and operation of the dam have had environmental and ecological consequences, including the displacement of communities and changes to the river's ecology. Efforts are made to mitigate these impacts through various conservation and resettlement programs.

7. Yangtze River Cruises:

- Many tourists visit the Three Gorges Dam as part of their Yangtze River cruise experience. Cruises often include stops at the dam, providing passengers with the opportunity to see this impressive engineering marvel up close.

8. Visitor Center:

- The Three Gorges Dam Visitor Center offers exhibitions and information about the dam's construction and its significance. Visitors can learn about the project's history, impact, and technology.

The Three Gorges Dam represents a significant achievement in engineering and infrastructure development, and it has had a transformative impact on the Yangtze River region. It's a place where you can learn about China's commitment to harnessing renewable energy, flood control efforts, and environmental conservation initiatives.

Dazu Rock Carvings

The Dazu Rock Carvings are a remarkable collection of Buddhist, Confucian, and Taoist stone sculptures and carvings that date back over a thousand years. Located in Dazu County, Chongqing, these intricate carvings are a UNESCO World Heritage site and one of China's most significant cultural and religious treasures. Here's what you need to know about the Dazu Rock Carvings:

1. Location:

- The Dazu Rock Carvings are located in Dazu County, which is part of Chongqing Municipality. It's situated about 160 kilometers (100 miles) from the city center of Chongqing, making it a popular day trip or weekend getaway for visitors to the region.

2. History:

- The carvings at Dazu date back to the 9th to 13th centuries during the Tang and Song dynasties, with some later additions from the Ming and Qing dynasties. They were created over centuries by Buddhist monks and artists and represent a rich fusion of Buddhism, Confucianism, and Taoism.

3. Styles and Themes:

- The carvings are diverse in style and content, with depictions of Buddha statues, bodhisattvas, gods, scenes from Buddhist and Taoist mythology, and even secular scenes illustrating daily life during the periods in which they were created.

4. Notable Sites:

- The Dazu Rock Carvings are divided into several sites, each with its own unique character. Notable sites include Baodingshan, Beishan, Nanshan, Shimenshan, and Shizhuanshan. Baodingshan, in particular, is known for its well-preserved and intricately detailed sculptures.

5. UNESCO World Heritage:

- In 1999, the Dazu Rock Carvings were designated as a UNESCO World Heritage site. This recognition acknowledges their cultural and historical significance.

6. Artistic Expression:

- The carvings showcase the artistic skills of the time and provide insights into the religious and philosophical beliefs of the people in ancient China. The intricate carvings reflect the creativity and devotion of the artists who created them.

7. Accessibility:

- The Dazu Rock Carvings are accessible to visitors through guided tours and well-maintained paths. While some carvings are located in caves, others are open-air and can be viewed easily.

8. Visitor Center:

- The Dazu Rock Carvings Visitor Center offers detailed information about the history and significance of the carvings. Visitors can learn about the artistry, historical context, and conservation efforts.

9. Cultural Experience:

- A visit to the Dazu Rock Carvings provides not only an opportunity to appreciate ancient art but also to gain insights into Chinese culture, religion, and history.

The Dazu Rock Carvings are a testament to the cultural and artistic achievements of ancient China. Exploring these carvings allows visitors to appreciate the interplay of religion, art, and history in one of China's most stunning cultural heritage sites.

Chongqing Zoo and Aquarium

The Chongqing Zoo and Aquarium is a popular destination for both locals and tourists in Chongqing. It offers a diverse collection of animals, marine life, and educational exhibits. Here's what you can expect when visiting the Chongqing Zoo and Aquarium:

1. Chongqing Zoo:

- The Chongqing Zoo is a comprehensive zoo with a wide range of animals from around the world. It's a great place for families and animal enthusiasts.

2. Animals:

- The zoo features a variety of animals, including giant pandas, red pandas, elephants, tigers, lions, giraffes, zebras, kangaroos, and numerous species of primates, birds, and reptiles.

3. Panda House:

- One of the highlights of the Chongqing Zoo is the Panda House, where you can see giant pandas up close. The zoo has been successful in breeding these endangered animals.

4. Animal Encounters:

- Some sections of the zoo offer opportunities for animal encounters and feeding experiences, particularly with smaller animals like goats and birds.

5. Education and Conservation:

- The zoo also focuses on education and conservation efforts. Visitors can learn about the animals, their habitats, and the importance of wildlife conservation.

6. Aquarium:

- The Chongqing Zoo and Aquarium includes an aquarium with a range of marine life. You can explore exhibits with fish, sharks, jellyfish, and other sea creatures.

7. Giant Panda House:

- In addition to the Panda House in the zoo, there's a separate Giant Panda House within the aquarium, where you can see more giant pandas and learn about their conservation.

8. Dolphin and Sea Lion Shows:

- The aquarium often hosts entertaining dolphin and sea lion shows, providing an interactive and educational experience for visitors.

9. Education and Research:

- The Chongqing Zoo and Aquarium actively engages in research and educational activities. They work to raise awareness about animal conservation and the importance of protecting biodiversity.

10. Convenient Location:

- The zoo and aquarium are conveniently located in the city, making it easily accessible for visitors. It's a popular spot for both locals and tourists.

The Chongqing Zoo and Aquarium offer a fun and educational experience for visitors of all ages. It's a great place to observe a wide variety of animals and learn about wildlife conservation efforts. If you're a fan of pandas, the opportunity to see these iconic creatures up close is a definite highlight.

Eling Park

Eling Park, also known as Eling Ridge Park or Yuzhong Park, is a picturesque urban park located in the Yuzhong District of Chongqing, China. It's a well-maintained and historically significant park that offers visitors a tranquil escape from the hustle and bustle of the city. Here's what you can expect when visiting Eling Park:

1. Scenic Location:

- Eling Park is perched on a hill, providing panoramic views of the Yangtze River and the city of Chongqing. The elevated location offers stunning vistas, especially during sunset.

2. Historical Significance:

- The park has a rich history dating back to the late Qing Dynasty (late 19th century). It was originally built as a private garden and later opened to the public.

3. Landscaped Gardens:

- Eling Park is beautifully landscaped with lush gardens, colorful flower beds, and meandering paths. The park is known for its well-maintained greenery, making it a serene place to relax and take leisurely strolls.

4. Architectural Features:

- The park features various pavilions, bridges, and statues, including the historic White Emperor's Pavilion, which is a prominent landmark within the park.

5. White Emperor's Pavilion:

- The White Emperor's Pavilion is a historical building located at the highest point of the park. It's a classical-style pavilion with intricate architecture and is a great spot to capture panoramic views of the city.

6. Teahouses and Cafes:

- Eling Park is home to several teahouses and cafes where you can enjoy a cup of tea or coffee while taking in the serene surroundings.

7. Relaxation and Recreation:

- Visitors can engage in relaxation, leisure activities, and picnics in the park. It's a popular spot for locals and tourists to unwind and enjoy the natural beauty.

8. Cultural Activities:

- The park occasionally hosts cultural events, performances, and art exhibitions, adding to its cultural appeal.

9. Accessibility:

- Eling Park is easily accessible by public transportation, and the park entrance is located in the city center, making it a convenient destination for visitors.

10. Photographers' Delight:

· The park's scenic beauty, traditional architecture, and panoramic views make it a favorite location for photographers and artists.

Eling Park is a peaceful oasis in the heart of Chongqing, offering a blend of natural beauty, historical charm, and cultural significance. Whether you're seeking a quiet place to relax, enjoy scenic views, or explore historical sites, Eling Park is a delightful destination for visitors of all ages.

Cultural Experiences

Chongqing offers a range of cultural experiences that allow you to immerse yourself in the city's rich history and traditions. Here are some cultural experiences you can enjoy in Chongqing:

1. Traditional Sichuan Opera:

· Watch a Sichuan Opera performance, which often includes face-changing (bian lian) acts, fire-spitting, and other traditional art forms. The Chongqing Guotai Arts Center is a popular venue for such performances.

2. Tea Tasting:

· Chongqing has a deep tea culture. Visit a traditional tea-house to savor local tea, learn about different tea varieties, and experience a traditional tea ceremony.

3. Tai Chi and Martial Arts:

· Join a Tai Chi or martial arts class in a local park. Tai Chi is a Chinese martial art that combines physical exercise with mindfulness and meditation.

4. Chongqing Hotpot Experience:

· Hotpot is an integral part of Chongqing's food culture. Join a hotpot cooking class to learn how to prepare and enjoy this fiery dish.

5. Calligraphy and Brush Painting:

· Enroll in a calligraphy or brush painting class to learn the basics of these traditional Chinese arts. You can create your own artwork or appreciate the skills of local artists.

6. Traditional Festivals:

· Plan your visit to coincide with traditional Chinese festivals, such as the Spring Festival (Chinese New Year), Lantern Festival, or Mid-Autumn Festival, to witness cultural celebrations, parades, and special events.

7. Visit Temples and Shrines:

- Explore Chongqing's temples and shrines, such as the Arhat Temple, Luohan Si, and Baiyun Guan Temple, to gain insights into Chinese Buddhism and Taoism.

8. Visit Old Towns:

- Wander through historic districts like Ciqikou Ancient Town to experience traditional architecture, local crafts, and cultural performances.

9. Local Markets:

- Explore local markets and street vendors to engage with artisans and purchase traditional crafts, souvenirs, and local products.

10. Cultural Museums:

- Visit cultural museums in Chongqing, such as the Chongqing China Three Gorges Museum, to learn about the history, culture, and heritage of the region.

11. Chinese Language and Calligraphy Classes:

- Enroll in language classes or calligraphy workshops to gain a deeper understanding of the Chinese language and its artistic expressions.

12. Chuan Opera:

- Chuan Opera is a traditional local opera in Chongqing,

known for its unique performances and music. Attend a Chuan Opera show to experience a distinctive form of Chinese opera.

13. Cultural Tours:

· Join guided cultural tours that explore Chongqing's history, traditions, and landmarks with the guidance of local experts.

14. Folk Performances:

· Seek out traditional folk performances and street artists in popular areas like Ciqikou and Hongyadong for an authentic taste of Chongqing's culture.

Chongqing's cultural experiences offer a glimpse into the city's rich heritage and traditions. Whether you're interested in the performing arts, visual arts, or traditional customs, there are numerous ways to engage with Chongqing's cultural essence.

Family-Friendly Activities

Chongqing offers a wide range of family-friendly activities and attractions that are sure to keep both kids and adults entertained. Here are some family-friendly activities to enjoy in Chongqing:

1. Chongqing Zoo:

· Visit the Chongqing Zoo to see a variety of animals, including giant pandas. It's an educational and fun experience for kids and adults alike.

2. Dazu Rock Carvings:

- Explore the ancient and intricate rock carvings at Dazu, which can be both educational and visually stimulating for children.

3. Chongqing Children's Palace:

- This cultural and recreational center offers a variety of activities for kids, including arts and crafts, music, and dance classes.

4. Eling Park:

- Take a family stroll through Eling Park's beautiful gardens and enjoy the serene atmosphere and scenic views of Chongqing.

5. Amusement Parks:

- Chongqing is home to several amusement parks, including Fantawild Adventure and Chongqing Happy Valley, which feature thrilling rides and entertainment.

6. Chongqing Science and Technology Museum:

- Engage kids in interactive learning at the Chongqing Science and Technology Museum, where they can explore science and technology exhibits.

7. Yangtze River Cruises:

- Enjoy a family-friendly cruise along the Yangtze River, offering scenic views and opportunities to see the Three Gorges Dam.

8. Chongqing Ocean Park:

- This marine-themed park has various aquatic exhibits and shows, including dolphin and sea lion performances.

9. Water Parks:

- Beat the summer heat at water parks like Caribbean Bay Water Park, where you can enjoy slides and pools.

10. Adventure Activities:

- Try thrilling activities such as ziplining, rock climbing, or indoor skydiving at Adventure Park Chongqing.

11. Local Festivals:

- Attend local festivals, such as Chinese New Year or Mid-Autumn Festival, where kids can enjoy traditional performances, lantern displays, and special events.

12. Chongqing Children's Art Troupe:

- Watch performances by the Chongqing Children's Art Troupe, showcasing the talents of young local artists.

13. Shopping and Dining:

- Explore family-friendly shopping districts like Jiefangbei Pedestrian Street and dine at restaurants with kids' menus and Western food options.

14. Hiking and Nature Exploration:

- Explore Chongqing's scenic natural areas, such as Gele Mountain National Forest Park, which offers family-friendly hiking and outdoor activities.

15. Art and Craft Workshops:

- Participate in art and craft workshops at local studios, where children can express their creativity.

Chongqing offers a diverse array of family-friendly activities, making it an excellent destination for a family vacation. Whether you're interested in nature, culture, or thrilling adventures, there's something for everyone to enjoy in Chongqing.

Off the Beaten Path

If you're looking to explore off the beaten path in Chongqing and discover hidden gems that may not be on every tourist's itinerary, here are some lesser-known places and experiences to consider:

1. Wulong Karst Landscape:

- Venture to Wulong County, a few hours outside of Chongqing, to explore the stunning karst landscapes. The Wulong Karst is a UNESCO World Heritage site known for its unique limestone formations, underground rivers, and natural bridges.

2. Tieshanping Forest Park:

- This lesser-visited forest park offers hiking trails, lush greenery, and serene natural beauty. It's a peaceful escape from the city's hustle and bustle.

3. Chongqing's Bookstores:

- Visit local bookstores like Zhang Jia Bookstore or Shui On's Bookstore for a quiet reading or browsing experience. These bookstores often host cultural events and book discussions.

4. Baiheliang Underwater Museum:

- Located near Wushan County, this underwater museum showcases ancient stone carvings submerged in the Yangtze

River. It's an archaeological site and a unique cultural attraction.

5. Diaoyu Fortress:

- Explore Diaoyu Fortress in the Shizhu Tujia Autonomous County. This ancient military fort is surrounded by pristine nature and offers a glimpse into local history.

6. Ronghui Hot Springs:

- Ronghui Hot Springs in Rongchang County is a tranquil retreat with various hot spring pools, lush gardens, and relaxation options.

7. Jigong Mountain:

- Located near Fuling District, Jigong Mountain is known for its beautiful scenery and hiking trails. It's a great spot for outdoor enthusiasts and nature lovers.

8. Chongqing Jiangbei Martyrs' Cemetery:

- Pay your respects at the Chongqing Jiangbei Martyrs' Cemetery, which commemorates those who sacrificed their lives during wartime. It's a place of historical significance.

9. Guoyuan Ancient Town:

- Visit Guoyuan Ancient Town, which has managed to retain its original charm with well-preserved buildings and a tranquil atmosphere.

10. Xiaonanhai Nature Reserve:

- Explore the Xiaonanhai Nature Reserve, home to diverse flora and fauna. It's a haven for birdwatching and nature photography.

11. Chongqing Forest Park:

- While not entirely off the beaten path, Chongqing Forest Park offers hiking trails, lush forests, and beautiful lakes, providing a peaceful escape from the city.

12. Small Villages Around Chongqing:

- Venture to small villages on the outskirts of Chongqing, where you can experience local customs, try authentic regional cuisine, and immerse yourself in rural life.

Exploring these off-the-beaten-path destinations in Chongqing will give you a unique and authentic perspective on the city and its surroundings, allowing you to discover hidden cultural and natural treasures.

7

Chapter 7

IMMERSING IN CHONGQING'S CULTURE

Local Festivals and Events

I mmersing in Chongqing's culture can be a rich and vibrant experience, and attending local festivals and events is an excellent way to do so. Here are some of the prominent festivals and events in Chongqing that offer a taste of the local culture:

1. Spring Festival (Chinese New Year):

- Celebrated with great enthusiasm, Spring Festival is China's most important traditional festival. In Chongqing, you can witness colorful parades, traditional lion and dragon dances, and the famous lantern displays.

2. Mid-Autumn Festival (Moon Festival):

- This festival is celebrated with mooncakes, lanterns, and family gatherings. You can explore traditional celebrations in the city's parks and public spaces.

3. Chongqing Hotpot Festival:

- A spicy culinary extravaganza celebrating Chongqing's signature dish, hotpot. During this event, you can sample various types of hotpot and enjoy cooking your own food at special gatherings.

4. Chongqing International Beer Festival:

- Held in August, this festival features a wide selection of beers, live music, and cultural performances. It's a great opportunity to enjoy the local and international beer scene.

5. Chongqing International Film and Video Festival:

- If you're a film enthusiast, this festival showcases a variety of films and provides opportunities to interact with film-makers and industry professionals.

6. Chongqing Dragon Boat Festival:

- Experience traditional dragon boat races and cultural performances during this festival, which commemorates the ancient poet Qu Yuan.

7. Chongqing Carnival:

- A vibrant event with parades, concerts, and a carnival atmosphere. It's a festive celebration that brings locals and tourists together.

8. Flower Festivals:

- Throughout the year, Chongqing hosts various flower festivals, including the Chongqing International Flower Expo, where you can enjoy beautiful floral displays and horticultural exhibitions.

9. Chongqing International Auto Consumer Festival:

- If you're interested in cars and automotive culture, this festival features exhibitions, test drives, and entertainment related to the automobile industry.

10. Traditional Temple Fairs: - Visit local temples during their annual fairs, where you can enjoy traditional performances, folk art, and local snacks. Notable temples in Chongqing include Arhat Temple and Baiyun Guan Temple.

11. Folk Performances: - Keep an eye out for street performances, traditional arts, and cultural shows in popular areas like Ciqikou Ancient Town and Hongyadong.

12. Chongqing Marathon: - If you're a runner or a sports enthusiast, consider participating in the Chongqing International Marathon or cheering on the participants.

Participating in these festivals and events allows you to engage with Chongqing's culture, experience local traditions, and mingle with both residents and fellow travelers. It's a wonderful way to embrace the city's vibrant and diverse cultural heritage.

Art and Performing Arts

Chongqing boasts a thriving arts and performing arts scene, with a variety of venues and events that cater to enthusiasts of visual and performing arts. Here are some ways to immerse yourself in the art and culture of Chongqing:

1. Chongqing Guotai Arts Center:

- This cultural complex hosts a range of performances, including Sichuan Opera with face-changing (bian lian) acts, traditional music, dance, and contemporary productions.

2. Chongqing Grand Theater:

- Located in the Jiefangbei area, the Chongqing Grand Theater hosts a diverse array of performances, including opera, ballet, drama, and concerts. The modern architecture of the theater is an attraction in itself.

3. Chongqing Jiangbei Theater:

- This theater features a variety of artistic performances, from traditional Chinese operas to contemporary stage productions.

4. Art Galleries and Museums:

- Visit art galleries such as the Chongqing Art Museum, where you can explore a range of contemporary and traditional Chinese artworks. The China Three Gorges Museum also hosts art exhibitions.

5. Chuan Opera:

- Experience the traditional Chuan Opera, which is unique to the Sichuan and Chongqing regions. It combines music, opera, and local folk culture.

6. Concerts and Live Music:

- Keep an eye out for live music events and concerts at venues like Nuts Live House and Little Bar. Chongqing has a growing indie music scene.

7. Street Performances:

- While exploring popular areas like Ciqikou Ancient Town and Hongyadong, you may encounter street performers, artists, and traditional acts showcasing their talents.

8. Chongqing Performing Arts Group:

- This group often stages productions, including traditional Chinese opera, dance, and music performances. Check their schedule for upcoming shows.

9. Chongqing Symphony Orchestra:

- Enjoy classical music performances by the Chongqing Symphony Orchestra, which frequently presents concerts featuring both Chinese and Western compositions.

10. Dance Performances: - Explore modern and traditional dance performances at various venues and theaters in Chongqing. Local and international dance troupes often visit the city.

11. Local Theater Productions: - Keep an eye out for local theater productions and community theaters, which may present original plays and performances.

12. Art and Calligraphy Workshops: - Enroll in art and calligraphy workshops to learn the basics of Chinese brush painting, calligraphy, and other traditional art forms.

13. Chongqing Youth Palace: - This cultural center frequently hosts youth-oriented arts and cultural events, from theater productions to art exhibitions.

Chongqing's arts and performing arts scene is a dynamic and evolving part of the city's cultural identity. Whether you're interested in traditional Chinese arts, contemporary performances, or visual arts, Chongqing has much to offer for art and culture enthusiasts.

Traditional Crafts

Traditional crafts in Chongqing reflect the city's rich cultural heritage and offer a glimpse into the skilled craftsmanship of the region. If you're interested in traditional crafts, here are some you can explore in Chongqing:

1. Ciqikou Porcelain: Ciqikou Ancient Town is renowned for its porcelain production. Visit local workshops and stores to see artisans creating beautiful porcelain pieces, from teacups to vases.

2. Embroidery: Chongqing is famous for its exquisite embroidery work. Visit embroidery shops and workshops to see skilled artisans creating intricate designs on silk and other fabrics.

3. Bamboo Weaving: Local artisans in Chongqing are skilled in bamboo weaving. You can find bamboo products like baskets, fans, and more at markets and traditional craft stores.

4. Inkstone Carving: Chongqing is known for its inkstone carving, which produces finely detailed inkstones used in Chinese calligraphy and painting. You can watch artisans at work and even purchase their creations.

5. Hand-painted Fans: Traditional hand-painted fans are a beautiful and functional craft. Explore markets and artisan shops to see the process and purchase hand-painted fans as souvenirs.

6. Paper Cutting: Chongqing is known for its intricate paper cutting art. You can find paper cuttings featuring various designs and themes. Some artisans may even offer paper cutting demonstrations.

7. Shadow Puppetry: Shadow puppetry is a traditional form of Chinese theater. While it's less common than in the past, you can still find shadow puppetry performances in some cultural venues.

8. Cloisonné Enamel: Cloisonné enamel is a craft that involves decorating metal objects with colorful enamels. While it's not as prevalent as some other crafts, you may come across cloisonné pieces in specialty stores.

9. Traditional Chinese Painting: Chongqing has a thriving art scene, and you can explore traditional Chinese painting at art galleries and studios. Some places offer painting workshops for visitors.

10. Calligraphy: Calligraphy is an important traditional art form in China. Attend calligraphy classes or visit calligraphy shops to appreciate the skill and artistry of local calligraphers.

11. Tea Ware: Chongqing has a strong tea culture, and you can find traditional tea ware, including teapots, cups, and tea sets. These make for both functional and decorative souvenirs.

12. Woven Silk Products: Chongqing is known for its silk production. You can purchase silk scarves, clothing, and other silk products at local markets and shops.

Exploring traditional crafts in Chongqing offers an opportunity to appreciate the artistry, culture, and history of the region. Many craft shops and markets in the city allow you to observe artisans at work and purchase handmade items as unique and meaningful souvenirs.

Language and Local Phrases

In Chongqing, as in many parts of China, the primary language spoken is Mandarin Chinese. However, due to its unique location and history, Chongqing has developed some regional dialect and expressions. Here are some local phrases and essential Chinese phrases to help you navigate and connect with locals:

Local Phrases:

1. **Chongqing Dialect Greeting:** When in Chongqing, you can use the local greeting "Chóngqìng hé niǔ," which means "Chongqing, hello!"
2. **Hotpot Orders:** If you're enjoying Chongqing hotpot, you can use these phrases:

- "Là de, bú yào tài là" () - "Spicy, but not too spicy."
- "Dān chǐ" () - "Egg drop" (for the hotpot).

Essential Chinese Phrases:

1. **Greetings:**

- "Nǐ hǎo" () – "Hello."
- "Zǎo shàng hǎo" () – "Good morning."
- "Wǎn shàng hǎo" () – "Good evening."
- "Xièxiè" () – "Thank you."
- "Duìbuqǐ" () – "Sorry."

1. **Common Phrases:**

- "Wǒ yào" () – "I want."
- "Tīng bù dǒng" () – "I don't understand."
- "Wǒ bù huì shuō zhōngwén" () – "I can't speak Chinese."

1. **Asking for Help:**

- "Néng bāng wǒ ma?" (?) – "Can you help me?"
- "Qǐng wèn..." (...) – "Excuse me..."

1. **Directions:**

- "Zěnme zǒu?" (?) – "How do I get there?"
- "Zuǒ guǎi" () – "Turn left."
- "Yòu guǎi" () – "Turn right."

1. **Numbers:**

- "Yī" () – "One"
- "Èr" () – "Two"
- "Sān" () – "Three"
- "Sì" () – "Four"
- "Wǔ" () – "Five"

1. **Food and Dining:**

- "Wǒ xiǎng diǎn zhè gè" () – "I would like to order this."
- "Bú yào là" () – "Not spicy."

Remember that the pronunciation of Chinese words can vary significantly, and a phrase spoken with the correct tones is crucial for understanding. Locals in Chongqing may appreciate your efforts to use the local dialect, but most will understand and respond to standard Mandarin Chinese. Learning some basic phrases in Mandarin will be especially helpful for communication during your visit to Chongqing.

Cultural Do's and Don'ts

When visiting Chongqing or any part of China, it's important to be aware of cultural norms and etiquette. Observing cultural do's and don'ts can enhance your experience and show respect for the local culture. Here are some cultural do's and don'ts for Chongqing and China in general:

Cultural Do's:

1. **Greet with Respect:** Greet people with a nod or a slight bow. It's common to address people by their title and last name, followed by "" (xiānsheng) for men or "" (nǚshì) for women.
2. **Use Both Hands:** When giving or receiving items, use both hands. It's a sign of respect.

3. **Accept Business Cards Gracefully:** If offered a business card, receive it with both hands, study it briefly, and express appreciation. Never write on or fold a business card.

4. **Use Chopsticks Properly:** When eating with chopsticks, do not point them at others or leave them sticking upright in your food. It's considered disrespectful.

5. **Remove Shoes Indoors:** When entering someone's home or a traditional-style restaurant, remove your shoes. Slippers may be provided.

6. **Show Respect for Elders:** In Chinese culture, respecting your elders is crucial. Use polite language and gestures when interacting with older individuals.

7. **Try Local Customs:** Be open to trying local customs and traditions. This can include participating in local festivals or trying traditional foods.

8. **Dress Modestly:** When visiting temples or sacred sites, dress modestly and cover your shoulders and knees. It's a sign of respect for the religious and cultural significance of these places.

9. **Respect Personal Space:** While Chongqing is a bustling city, respect personal space when standing in lines or navigating crowded areas.

Cultural Don'ts:

1. **Avoid Public Displays of Affection:** Public displays of affection, such as hugging and kissing, are generally not common in China. It's best to avoid them in public.

2. **Don't Point with Your Feet:** Pointing at people or objects

with your feet is considered impolite. Use your hand to gesture instead.

3. **Don't Touch People's Heads:** Touching someone's head, even playfully, is considered disrespectful in Chinese culture.

4. **Don't Discuss Sensitive Topics:** Avoid discussing sensitive topics like politics, religion, and human rights. These conversations can be uncomfortable for both you and your Chinese hosts.

5. **Don't Make Negative Gestures:** Avoid negative gestures like pointing with your index finger or making the "thumbs-down" sign. These can be offensive.

6. **Don't Finish All the Food:** In China, leaving a small amount of food on your plate indicates that you are full. Finishing all the food can be seen as a sign that you are still hungry and may prompt more servings.

7. **Don't Interrupt Others:** Interrupting people while they are speaking is considered rude. Let others finish speaking before you respond.

8. **Don't Bargain Aggressively:** While bargaining is common in markets, avoid aggressive or disrespectful haggling. Be polite and fair in negotiations.

9. **Don't Gift Clocks or White Flowers:** Gifting clocks or white flowers is associated with death and funerals in Chinese culture. Avoid these items as gifts.

By being mindful of these cultural do's and don'ts, you can show respect for local customs and traditions while enjoying your time in Chongqing and making positive cultural connections with the locals.

8

Chapter 8

SHOPPING AND SOUVENIRS

Shopping Districts

Chongqing offers a diverse shopping scene with various shopping districts catering to different tastes and preferences. Here are some of the most popular shopping districts and areas where you can find a wide range of goods and souvenirs:

1. Jiefangbei Pedestrian Street ( ):

- Located in the heart of downtown Chongqing, Jiefangbei is a bustling shopping district known for its vibrant atmosphere, modern shopping malls, department stores, and an array of boutiques. You can find a wide range of fashion, electronics, and local specialties.

2. Ciqikou Ancient Town ():

- Ciqikou, also known as Porcelain Village, is a historic and charming shopping district with cobbled streets and traditional architecture. It's a great place to shop for local crafts, porcelain, tea, and traditional snacks.

3. Guanyinqiao ():

- Guanyinqiao is a modern shopping and entertainment district in Chongqing, featuring large shopping malls, international brands, restaurants, and a vibrant nightlife scene.

4. Nanping Pedestrian Street ():

- Nanping is another popular shopping area in Chongqing with a wide range of shops, boutiques, and department stores. It's known for its variety of clothing, electronics, and street food.

5. Wulong Old Street ():

- Located in Wulong County, this old street is a great place to shop for traditional crafts, souvenirs, and local snacks. It's also near the famous Wulong Karst Landscape.

6. Yangjiaping ():

- Yangjiaping is a district that offers a mix of shopping options, from local markets to modern shopping centers. It's a good place to explore and find various items.

7. Three Gorges Square ():

- This square in Yuzhong District is home to several shopping centers, including Chongqing Department Store and Starlight 68 Plaza, where you can find clothing, electronics, and more.

8. Daping Shopping Area ():

- Daping is known for its electronics market, making it a good destination for tech enthusiasts looking for gadgets and electronics.

9. Longfor Paradise Walk ():

- This modern shopping complex offers a range of retail shops, restaurants, and entertainment options. It's a family-friendly shopping destination.

10. Wanda Plaza (): - Wanda Plaza is a chain of shopping and entertainment complexes in Chongqing, offering a variety of retail shops, dining options, and cinemas.

11. Hongyadong (): - While primarily known as a tourist attraction, Hongyadong also offers souvenir shops where you can find Chongqing-themed gifts, handicrafts, and traditional Chinese items.

Chongqing's shopping districts cater to all tastes, from luxury brands to local crafts and traditional items. Don't forget to haggle when shopping in markets and smaller shops, but be respectful and polite in your negotiations. When buying souvenirs, look for items such as Chongqing hotpot seasoning, traditional porcelain, Sichuan teas, and unique local crafts to bring back a piece of Chongqing's culture with you.

Markets and Bazaars

Chongqing offers a variety of markets and bazaars where you can shop for a wide range of goods, from fresh produce to clothing, antiques, and local crafts. Here are some notable markets and bazaars in Chongqing:

1. Chongqing Chaotianmen Market ( ):

- Located near the Chaotianmen Dock, this market is famous for its seafood, including a wide variety of live fish, seafood, and exotic delicacies. It's a bustling place to experience local food culture.

2. Jiaochangkou Shopping Street ( ):

- This historic market area in central Chongqing offers a mix of traditional shops, street vendors, and modern stores. You can find clothing, snacks, electronics, and local specialties.

3. Shapingba Night Market ( ):

- Operating mainly in the evenings, this night market is known for its street food and local delicacies. Try Chongqing hotpot, grilled skewers, and other Sichuan dishes.

4. Tongyuanmen Fresh Food Market ():

- This market is a great place to explore local ingredients, fresh produce, and an array of exotic foods used in Chongqing cuisine. It's a bustling and vibrant market.

5. Baiheliang Ancient Street ():

- Located in Wulong County, this ancient street features a variety of stalls and shops selling local crafts, antiques, and traditional Chinese souvenirs.

6. Yuzhong Night Market ():

- Yuzhong Night Market offers a lively atmosphere in the evenings, with street vendors selling snacks, clothing, and various items. It's a great place for night shopping.

7. Yangjiaping Secondhand Market ():

- If you're interested in vintage items and antiques, visit this secondhand market to find unique collectibles, old books, and more.

8. Guanyinqiao Antique Market ():

- This market specializes in antiques and vintage items, including porcelain, furniture, art, and curios. It's a good place for collectors and enthusiasts.

9. Beibei Flower and Bird Market ():

· Explore the Beibei Flower and Bird Market for a wide selection of plants, flowers, and small pets. It's a colorful and lively market.

10. Rongchang Ancient Market (): - Located in Rongchang County, this ancient market features traditional Chinese architecture and a variety of stalls selling local products, crafts, and snacks.

11. Ciqikou Antique Market (): - In addition to the ancient town's charm, Ciqikou has an antique market where you can find old coins, jewelry, and traditional Chinese collectibles.

Chongqing's markets and bazaars offer a wide range of shopping experiences, from traditional street markets to specialized antique markets. These markets are not only great places to shop but also opportunities to immerse yourself in the local culture and try Chongqing's famous street food.

Unique Souvenirs

When shopping for souvenirs in Chongqing, you'll find a wide array of unique items that reflect the city's culture, cuisine, and history. Here are some unique souvenirs to consider bringing back from your visit to Chongqing:

1. **Chongqing Hotpot Seasoning:** Chongqing is renowned for

its fiery hotpot. Consider purchasing authentic Chongqing hotpot seasoning blends to recreate the experience at home.

2. **Porcelain and Ceramics:** Ciqikou Ancient Town is a hub for porcelain and ceramic products. You can find beautifully hand-painted porcelain items like teapots, vases, and decorative pieces.

3. **Sichuan and Chongqing Teas:** Explore tea shops for a selection of high-quality teas, including Chongqing green tea and Sichuan jasmine tea. Teas are often beautifully packaged and make great gifts.

4. **Sichuan Pepper:** Known as "huajiao" in Chinese, Sichuan pepper is a key ingredient in Sichuan cuisine. You can purchase whole Sichuan peppercorns or ground spice blends.

5. **Traditional Chinese Paintings and Calligraphy:** Chongqing has a vibrant art scene, and you can find beautiful traditional Chinese paintings and calligraphy scrolls that make elegant souvenirs.

6. **Local Crafts:** Look for handcrafted items such as bamboo products, traditional paper cuts, and embroidered silk handkerchiefs. These showcase local craftsmanship and artistry.

7. **Chinese Knots:** Chinese knots, known as "jié," are intricate decorative knots that symbolize good luck and happiness. They come in various designs and can be used as ornaments or accessories.

8. **Traditional Sichuan Opera Masks:** Chongqing and Sichuan are known for their unique opera styles. Collect traditional Sichuan opera masks as art pieces or wall decor.

9. **Cloisonné Enamelware:** Cloisonné enamelware combines

metalwork with colorful enamel designs. Look for unique jewelry, vases, or decorative pieces.

10. **Panda-Themed Souvenirs:** While pandas are not native to Chongqing, they are popular in China. You can find panda-themed items, such as plush toys, keychains, and accessories.

11. **Chongqing Map Art:** Local artists often create maps of Chongqing as artwork. These can be a unique and artistic memento of your trip.

12. **Spicy Snacks:** Chongqing is famous for its spicy snacks. Consider buying bags of "mala" (spicy and numbing) snacks to share with friends or enjoy at home.

13. **Regional Liquor:** Try Baijiu, a strong Chinese liquor, or explore local liqueurs flavored with herbs and spices unique to the region.

14. **Traditional Chinese Fans:** Decorative fans are a classic Chinese souvenir. Look for intricately designed hand fans that showcase traditional Chinese motifs.

15. **Antique and Vintage Finds:** Antique markets in Chongqing offer unique collectibles, old coins, and vintage items that can be excellent conversation starters and reminders of your visit.

When selecting souvenirs, consider the tastes and interests of the recipients and look for items that have a personal connection to your Chongqing experience. Shopping in the city's markets and stores allows you to explore the local culture and bring home distinctive mementos.

Bargaining Tips

Bargaining is a common practice in many markets and smaller shops in Chongqing, as it is in many parts of China. While it's a cultural norm, it's essential to approach bargaining with respect and politeness. Here are some bargaining tips to help you navigate the process successfully:

1. Start with a Smile:

- Begin with a friendly and polite demeanor. A smile can go a long way in creating a positive atmosphere for negotiations.

2. Do Your Research:

- Before you start bargaining, research the approximate price range for the item you're interested in. This will give you a reasonable starting point for negotiations.

3. Be Polite and Respectful:

- Maintain a respectful tone throughout the bargaining process. Address the seller with courteous phrases like "Nǐ hǎo" (hello) and "Xièxiè" (thank you).

4. Use Nonverbal Communication:

- When stating your desired price or showing reluctance, use nonverbal cues like body language, facial expressions, and hand gestures. This can convey your message effectively.

5. Counteroffer:

- After the seller names their price, counter with a lower but reasonable offer. This begins the back-and-forth negotiation.

6. Be Patient:

- Bargaining can take time, so be patient and prepared to spend a few minutes working out a deal. Don't rush the process.

7. Show Willingness to Walk Away:

- Be ready to walk away if you're not satisfied with the final price. This can sometimes encourage the seller to offer a better deal.

8. Engage in Friendly Banter:

- Bargaining is often a social activity in China. Engage in friendly banter, ask about the seller's day, and show genuine interest. This can help build rapport.

9. Bundle Purchases:

- If you're buying multiple items from the same vendor, consider bundling them together for a discount. Sellers may be more willing to offer a deal for larger purchases.

10. Don't Overdo It: - While bargaining is expected, avoid being overly aggressive or haggling to the point of discomfort. Balance assertiveness with respect.

11. Know When to Stop: - Once you and the seller reach a price you're comfortable with, it's good practice to stop negotiating and make the purchase.

12. Respect Local Customs: - Keep in mind that in some markets or for certain items, prices may already be quite low. In such cases, it's considerate to accept the initial offer without haggling.

Remember that successful bargaining should result in a fair price for both you and the seller. It's a customary and enjoyable part of the shopping experience in Chongqing, and it can be a fun way to interact with local vendors and learn more about the local culture.

9

Chapter 9

CHONGQING'S NIGHTLIFE

Night Markets

C hongqing's nightlife scene comes alive after dark, offering a mix of entertainment, dining, and unique experiences. While Chongqing doesn't have traditional night markets in the same way you might find in some other Chinese cities, it has a vibrant evening scene with nightclubs, bars, and street food stalls. Here are some areas and locations to explore Chongqing's nightlife:

1. **Jiefangbei ():**

- Chongqing's central business district, Jiefangbei, offers a variety of entertainment options, including bars, nightclubs, and late-night street food vendors. It's a popular area for both locals and tourists.

1. **Yangtze River Cruises:**

- Enjoy a nighttime cruise along the Yangtze River, which offers stunning views of the city's illuminated skyline. Many cruise operators provide dinner and entertainment on board.

1. **Hongyadong ():**

- Hongyadong is a popular attraction and nightlife hub. It's known for its unique architectural design and features restaurants, bars, and souvenir shops. The area is beautifully lit up in the evening.

1. **Nanbin Road ():**

- Nanbin Road is famous for its riverside bars and restaurants. You can enjoy a drink with a view of the river and the city's skyline. It's a great place for a leisurely evening.

1. **Guanyinqiao ():**

- Guanyinqiao is a bustling area with numerous bars, clubs, and entertainment venues. It's a popular choice for those seeking a lively nightlife experience.

1. **Daping and Jiangbei Districts:**

- These areas have several nightclubs and karaoke bars, making them good choices for partygoers.

1. **Ciqikou Ancient Town ():**

- While primarily a daytime destination, Ciqikou also has some evening entertainment options, including traditional performances and local snacks.

1. **Shapingba Night Market ():**

- Although it's known for its street food, Shapingba Night Market also has a vibrant atmosphere with stalls selling local delicacies.

1. **Live Music Venues:** Chongqing has a growing live music scene with venues like Nuts Live House and Little Bar, where you can enjoy performances by local and international bands.
2. **The Bund Plaza ():**

- Located on the Chongqing Peninsula, The Bund Plaza is a popular spot for an evening stroll, offering picturesque views of the riverside area.

1. **Wine Bars and Rooftop Bars:** Explore the city's upscale wine bars and rooftop bars for a more relaxed and elegant evening experience.
2. **Late-Night Snacking:** Chongqing is famous for its late-night street food, particularly spicy snacks. Look for local vendors offering skewers, fried chicken, and other delicacies.

Chongqing's nightlife scene caters to a wide range of tastes, from those seeking a vibrant party atmosphere to those looking for a more relaxed evening by the riverside. Keep in mind that Chongqing is known for its spicy cuisine, so be prepared for some fiery late-night snacks to go along with your drinks and entertainment.

· Bars and Clubs

Chongqing has a lively nightlife scene, with a variety of bars and clubs to suit different tastes. Here are some popular bars and clubs in Chongqing where you can enjoy a night out:

Bars:

1. **Monkey Bar ():** Located in the Jiefangbei district, this rooftop bar offers stunning views of the city skyline. It's known for its craft cocktails and relaxed atmosphere.
2. **Seventh Heaven ():** A stylish lounge bar in the Jiefangbei area, Seventh Heaven is a great spot for cocktails, live music, and a sophisticated ambiance.
3. **Hemingway's Bar:** This popular expat bar in the Shapingba district serves a range of beers, cocktails, and pub food. It often hosts events and live music.
4. **Soho Bar:** Located in Guanyinqiao, Soho Bar is known for its lively atmosphere, live bands, and a dance floor for those who want to groove to the music.
5. **Regent Club ():** A well-known venue for live music and dancing, Regent Club is a popular destination for partygoers in Chongqing.

Clubs:

1. **Angel Club ( ):** One of Chongqing's largest and most famous nightclubs, Angel Club features top DJs, a spacious dance floor, and a lively party atmosphere.
2. **Monkey Livehouse:** For a dose of live music and dancing, Monkey Livehouse in the Jiefangbei area often hosts bands and DJs, making it a vibrant nightlife spot.
3. **VV Bar & Club (VV):** Located near Chongqing University, VV Bar & Club offers a mix of EDM and hip-hop music, a spacious dance floor, and a trendy crowd.
4. **Morning Bar ( ):** A popular club with a focus on electronic music and DJ performances, Morning Bar is a go-to destination for electronic dance music enthusiasts.
5. **Cocoa Club ( ):** Situated in Guanyinqiao, Cocoa Club is known for its high-energy parties and a variety of music genres, including hip-hop and EDM.
6. **Lan Kwai Fong ( ):** Inspired by the famous nightlife district in Hong Kong, Chongqing's Lan Kwai Fong offers a concentration of bars, clubs, and restaurants in the Jiefangbei area.
7. **Block 3 Club ( ):** Located in the Shapingba district, Block 3 Club is known for its energetic atmosphere and a diverse lineup of DJs.

Please note that the nightlife scene in Chongqing can change, and new venues may open over time. It's a good idea to check for current information and events if you plan to visit specific bars or clubs during your stay. Also, remember to be aware of local customs and alcohol regulations when enjoying the nightlife in Chongqing.

Live Music Venues

Chongqing has a lively nightlife scene, with a variety of bars and clubs to suit different tastes. Here are some popular bars and clubs in Chongqing where you can enjoy a night out:

Bars:

1. **Monkey Bar ():** Located in the Jiefangbei district, this rooftop bar offers stunning views of the city skyline. It's known for its craft cocktails and relaxed atmosphere.
2. **Seventh Heaven ():** A stylish lounge bar in the Jiefangbei area, Seventh Heaven is a great spot for cocktails, live music, and a sophisticated ambiance.
3. **Hemingway's Bar:** This popular expat bar in the Shapingba district serves a range of beers, cocktails, and pub food. It often hosts events and live music.
4. **Soho Bar:** Located in Guanyinqiao, Soho Bar is known for its lively atmosphere, live bands, and a dance floor for those who want to groove to the music.
5. **Regent Club ():** A well-known venue for live music and dancing, Regent Club is a popular destination for partygoers in Chongqing.

Clubs:

1. **Angel Club ():** One of Chongqing's largest and most famous nightclubs, Angel Club features top DJs, a spacious dance floor, and a lively party atmosphere.
2. **Monkey Livehouse:** For a dose of live music and dancing, Monkey Livehouse in the Jiefangbei area often hosts bands

and DJs, making it a vibrant nightlife spot.

3. **VV Bar & Club (VV):** Located near Chongqing University, VV Bar & Club offers a mix of EDM and hip-hop music, a spacious dance floor, and a trendy crowd.

4. **Morning Bar ():** A popular club with a focus on electronic music and DJ performances, Morning Bar is a go-to destination for electronic dance music enthusiasts.

5. **Cocoa Club ():** Situated in Guanyinqiao, Cocoa Club is known for its high-energy parties and a variety of music genres, including hip-hop and EDM.

6. **Lan Kwai Fong ():** Inspired by the famous nightlife district in Hong Kong, Chongqing's Lan Kwai Fong offers a concentration of bars, clubs, and restaurants in the Jiefangbei area.

7. **Block 3 Club ():** Located in the Shapingba district, Block 3 Club is known for its energetic atmosphere and a diverse lineup of DJs.

Please note that the nightlife scene in Chongqing can change, and new venues may open over time. It's a good idea to check for current information and events if you plan to visit specific bars or clubs during your stay. Also, remember to be aware of local customs and alcohol regulations when enjoying the nightlife in Chongqing.

Evening Cruises

Evening cruises in Chongqing offer a unique way to enjoy the city's stunning skyline and the glittering lights of the Yangtze and Jialing Rivers. Here are some options for evening cruises in Chongqing:

1. **Yangtze River Night Cruise:** An evening cruise on the Yangtze River is a fantastic way to see Chongqing's skyline illuminated at night. Many operators offer cruises with dinner, live entertainment, and panoramic views of the city's landmarks, including the Hongya Cave and Chaotianmen Dock.

2. **Jialing River Night Cruise:** The Jialing River flows through Chongqing, and a night cruise along this river provides a different perspective of the city. You can enjoy the beautiful reflections of the city's lights in the water.

3. **Luxury Dinner Cruises:** Several companies offer luxury dinner cruises on both the Yangtze and Jialing Rivers. These cruises typically include a sumptuous dinner, live music, and a romantic ambiance.

4. **Traditional Wooden Boat Tours:** For a more traditional experience, you can take a ride on a wooden boat. These smaller boats often travel along the rivers in the evening, offering a peaceful and charming cruise.

5. **Themed Cruises:** Some cruise operators offer themed cruises with unique experiences. These can include themed parties, cultural performances, and more.

6. **Private Charter Cruises:** If you're looking for a more personalized experience, you can charter a private boat for a romantic evening, a special event, or a small group

gathering.

7. **Chaotianmen Dock:** This is a popular departure point for many night cruises. It's also a great spot to enjoy the city's waterfront views before or after your cruise.

8. **Online Booking:** You can often book your cruise online through various tour operators or travel agencies. Be sure to check the details, including the cruise duration, inclusions, and the departure point.

Evening cruises in Chongqing provide a serene and picturesque way to take in the city's beauty after dark. Be sure to choose a cruise that suits your preferences, whether you're looking for a romantic dinner on the water or simply a peaceful and scenic tour of the city's lights. Don't forget to bring your camera to capture the stunning views.

Entertainment and Shows

Chongqing offers a variety of entertainment and shows for visitors to enjoy. Whether you're interested in traditional Chinese performances, modern theater, or cultural experiences, there are options to suit a range of interests. Here are some entertainment and show options in Chongqing:

1. **Chongqing Grand Theatre ():** This modern theater hosts a variety of performances, including opera, ballet, musicals, and concerts. It's a great place to enjoy high-quality cultural shows.

2. **Sichuan Opera:** Sichuan Opera is a traditional Chinese

performance that combines face-changing (Bian Lian), fire-spitting, and other dramatic acts. You can watch Sichuan Opera shows at various venues in Chongqing, including Hongyadong and the Chongqing Guotai Arts Center.

3. **Three Gorges Tourism Culture Square ():** Located near the Three Gorges Dam, this cultural square often hosts folk performances and traditional Chinese shows that showcase the local culture of the Three Gorges region.

4. **Wulong Karst Landscape:**

- While not a traditional entertainment venue, the Wulong Karst Landscape is a UNESCO World Heritage site that has been the backdrop for numerous film and television productions. You can explore the natural beauty of the area and take guided tours to learn about its history.

1. **Red Theater ():** The Red Theater is known for its "The Legend of Kung Fu" show, which combines martial arts, dance, and acrobatics to tell the story of a young boy's journey to becoming a Kung Fu master.

2. **Chongqing Puppet Theatre ():** If you're interested in traditional puppetry, the Chongqing Puppet Theatre hosts performances featuring different types of puppetry, such as shadow puppetry and hand puppetry.

3. **Bars and Clubs:** As mentioned earlier, Chongqing has a lively nightlife scene with bars and clubs that often host live music, DJ sets, and dance performances, providing entertainment well into the night.

4. **Local Festivals and Events:** Keep an eye on Chongqing's event calendar for special festivals and events, such as the

Chongqing Hotpot Festival or lantern festivals, which often feature cultural performances and entertainment.

5. **Hotpot Dinner Shows:** Some hotpot restaurants in Chongqing offer interactive dining experiences where you can enjoy a hotpot meal while watching live performances, such as Sichuan opera or traditional music.

6. **Cruise Entertainment:** Evening cruises on the Yangtze and Jialing Rivers often include live music, cultural performances, and other entertainment to enhance the experience.

Be sure to check the schedules and availability of specific shows or events during your visit to Chongqing, as performance schedules may vary. Whether you're interested in traditional Chinese culture or modern entertainment, you can find a variety of options to enjoy in this vibrant city.

Chapter 10

OUTDOOR ACTIVITIES

Hiking and Nature Parks

Chongqing, known for its unique mountainous terrain and natural beauty, offers excellent opportunities for outdoor activities, including hiking and exploration of nature parks. Here are some notable options for hiking and outdoor adventures in and around Chongqing:

1. **Wulong Karst Landscape ():** The Wulong Karst Landscape is a UNESCO World Heritage site located about 130 kilometers (81 miles) from Chongqing's city center. It's renowned for its stunning karst formations, deep canyons, and lush forests. Hiking in Wulong allows you to explore natural wonders like Furong Cave and the Three Natural Bridges. The hiking trails are well-marked, and you can choose from various levels of difficulty to suit your fitness and

experience.

2. **Jinfo Mountain ():** Located about 60 kilometers (37 miles) southwest of Chongqing, Jinfo Mountain is known for its serene beauty, ancient temples, and bamboo forests. The mountain offers various hiking trails, including the popular route to the summit. Along the way, you can enjoy scenic views of bamboo groves, waterfalls, and the Golden Buddha Temple.

3. **Chongqing Wuling Mountain National Park ():** Wuling Mountain National Park is situated in the Wuling Mountain Range in Chongqing's northern suburbs. It's a fantastic destination for hiking and exploring lush forests, unique rock formations, and pristine rivers. The park offers a range of hiking trails, from easy walks to more challenging routes.

4. **Chongqing Simian Mountain National Forest Park ():** Simian Mountain, located in the Simian Mountain National Forest Park, is known for its diverse flora and fauna, waterfalls, and stunning landscapes. Hiking trails take you through lush forests and offer breathtaking panoramic views of the surrounding area.

5. **Fengdu Ghost City ():** While famous for its cultural and historical significance, Fengdu Ghost City also offers hiking opportunities. The city is known for its unique ancient architecture and temples that tell the story of the afterlife. The scenic trails in the area lead to different parts of the city, providing an educational and picturesque hiking experience.

6. **Dazu Rock Carvings ():** While the Dazu Rock Carvings themselves are not for hiking, the surrounding areas offer beautiful natural scenery and hiking trails. The carvings

are a UNESCO World Heritage site and feature thousands of Buddhist, Taoist, and Confucian rock carvings.

7. **Changshou Lake Scenic Area ():** Located about 50 kilometers (31 miles) from the city center, Changshou Lake offers hiking trails along the picturesque lakeshore, with opportunities for boating and picnicking as well.

8. **Chongqing Botanical Garden ():** This botanical garden provides a serene and green escape within the city. You can explore walking trails through various themed gardens, which feature a wide array of plant species and offer a peaceful environment for a leisurely stroll.

When embarking on hiking and outdoor activities in Chongqing, it's essential to check the weather conditions, wear appropriate clothing and footwear, and bring essential supplies such as water, snacks, and a map or GPS device. Depending on the season, be prepared for varying temperatures and rain. It's also advisable to inform someone of your hiking plans and expected return time for safety. With its diverse natural landscapes, Chongqing offers a wide range of outdoor adventures for nature enthusiasts and hikers.

Water Activities

Chongqing, known for its proximity to the confluence of the Yangtze and Jialing Rivers, provides several water-based activities and experiences. Whether you're interested in cruising, rafting, or simply enjoying riverside views, here are some water activities to consider in Chongqing:

1. **Yangtze River Cruises:** A Yangtze River cruise is one of the most popular water-based activities in Chongqing. You can embark on multi-day cruises that take you through the beautiful Three Gorges, offering stunning views of the river's dramatic landscapes and the chance to explore local culture along the way. Cruises often include onboard accommodations, meals, and shore excursions to places like Fengdu Ghost City and the Lesser Three Gorges.

2. **Jialing River Cruises:** The Jialing River, a tributary of the Yangtze, flows through Chongqing. Short Jialing River cruises are available and provide a different perspective of the city's skyline. You can enjoy a leisurely boat ride and take in the scenery along the riverbanks.

3. **White Water Rafting:** Chongqing's surrounding areas, especially in the Wulong Karst Landscape and other mountainous regions, offer opportunities for white water rafting. These thrilling adventures take you down fast-flowing rivers and through scenic gorges.

4. **Paddle Boating and Kayaking:** Some areas along the rivers in Chongqing offer paddle boating and kayaking experiences. You can rent a paddle boat or kayak to explore the waterways at a more relaxed pace.

5. **Fishing:** Fishing enthusiasts can enjoy a day of angling on the Yangtze River. Local operators offer fishing excursions with the opportunity to catch a variety of fish species native to the region.

6. **Waterside Strolls and Cycling:** Chongqing's riverside areas often have walking and cycling paths. You can enjoy leisurely strolls or bike rides along the riverbanks while taking in the scenic views.

7. **Chongqing Chaotianmen Dock:** The Chaotianmen Dock

is a bustling area where you can watch ships, boats, and ferries come and go. It's an excellent spot for people-watching, enjoying river views, and experiencing the vibrant atmosphere of the riverside.

8. **Ferry Rides:** Chongqing has several ferry routes that provide convenient and affordable transportation across the rivers. You can use ferries to explore different parts of the city while enjoying a scenic journey.

9. **Dragon Boat Races:** During traditional festivals and special events, dragon boat races are held on the rivers. These races are a cultural spectacle and can be an exciting event to watch.

10. **Hiking and Waterside Picnics:** Many hiking trails in the region lead to beautiful waterside locations where you can enjoy picnics and relaxation by the riverbanks.

Before participating in water activities, it's essential to consider safety measures, weather conditions, and any necessary permits or permissions. Many of these activities are seasonal, so it's a good idea to check availability during your visit to Chongqing. Whether you're seeking adventure or a peaceful day by the water, Chongqing's water activities offer something for every traveler.

Parks and Gardens

Chongqing boasts a variety of parks and gardens that provide a welcome escape from the hustle and bustle of city life. These green spaces offer opportunities for relaxation, outdoor activities, and exploration. Here are some of the most notable parks and gardens in Chongqing:

1. **Hongya Cave Park ():** This park is located around the famous Hongya Cave complex, perched on the banks of the Jialing River. The park features beautifully landscaped gardens, terraces, and walking paths with panoramic views of the river and city.

2. **Nanshan Botanical Garden ():** Nanshan Botanical Garden is a serene oasis featuring a wide variety of plant species, thematic gardens, and walking trails. It's an ideal place for leisurely strolls and exploring the diverse flora of the region.

3. **Chongqing Zoo ():** Chongqing Zoo is not only a wildlife park but also a lovely place for a leisurely walk. You can explore the zoo's beautifully landscaped gardens and enjoy the company of animals from around the world.

4. **Chongqing Amusement Park ():** In addition to its thrilling rides, Chongqing Amusement Park offers lush green areas, gardens, and a serene lake where you can relax and enjoy a peaceful atmosphere.

5. **Bijin Park ():** This park is situated on the southern bank of the Yangtze River and features an attractive waterfront promenade, manicured gardens, and a beautiful Lotus Lake. It's an ideal place for a leisurely stroll.

6. **Eling Park ():** Eling Park is a historic park known for its gardens, pavilions, and scenic overlooks. It provides a tranquil escape from the city and offers stunning views of Chongqing's skyline.

7. **Chaotianmen Park ():** This park is located near Chaotianmen Dock and offers riverside gardens, walking paths, and recreational areas. It's a great spot to enjoy the river views

and watch the bustling river traffic.

8. **Fengdu Ghost City ():** Besides its cultural attractions, Fengdu Ghost City has beautifully landscaped gardens and areas where you can explore, relax, and enjoy the serene surroundings.

9. **Chongqing People's Square ():** Located in the city center, People's Square is a bustling urban park with gardens, sculptures, and a large plaza. It's a hub for events, cultural activities, and leisurely walks.

10. **Yangren Street Park ():** This park is situated in Yangren Street, a historical and cultural district. The park features green spaces, ponds, and gardens, making it a pleasant place for a quiet escape.

Chongqing's parks and gardens offer opportunities for both relaxation and exploration. Whether you're looking for a peaceful place to unwind or want to take a leisurely walk in beautiful surroundings, these green spaces provide a welcome respite from the urban environment.

Adventure Sports

Chongqing offers a variety of adventure sports and outdoor activities for thrill-seekers and outdoor enthusiasts. Whether you're interested in rock climbing, zip-lining, or off-road adventures, there are plenty of opportunities to get your adrenaline pumping. Here are some adventure sports to consider in Chongqing:

1. **Rock Climbing:** Chongqing has several rock climbing areas, including crags and indoor climbing gyms. Places like "Shapingba Climbing Gym" offer indoor climbing walls suitable for climbers of all skill levels. Outdoor climbing locations can be found in the surrounding mountains.

2. **Zip-Lining:** If you're looking for an exciting zip-lining experience, you can find options in Chongqing. Some attractions, such as the Wulong Karst Landscape, offer zip-line adventures that let you soar over stunning natural landscapes.

3. **Paragliding:** Chongqing's mountainous terrain provides ideal conditions for paragliding. There are paragliding clubs and instructors in the region who offer tandem flights for beginners and more experienced paragliders.

4. **White Water Rafting:** Chongqing's mountain rivers, such as those in the Wulong Karst Landscape, provide opportunities for thrilling white water rafting experiences. Experienced guides lead rafting trips down fast-flowing rivers.

5. **Mountain Biking:** The mountainous terrain around Chongqing is excellent for mountain biking. You can explore scenic trails and forested areas, either on your own or with local biking groups.

6. **ATV and Off-Roading:** Off-roading enthusiasts can find places in the Chongqing area where they can rent all-terrain vehicles (ATVs) and explore rugged trails.

7. **Canyoning:** Canyoning involves descending through waterfalls, streams, and steep canyons. Chongqing's natural landscapes provide opportunities for canyoning adventures, with local guides leading tours.

8. **Bungee Jumping:** Some adventure parks and attractions,

like Wansheng Black Valley Scenic Area, offer bungee jumping experiences from high platforms, providing a heart-pounding thrill.

9. **Hang Gliding:** If you're interested in hang gliding, you can find instructors and facilities in the Chongqing region that offer tandem flights and training for enthusiasts.

10. **Cave Exploration:** Chongqing is known for its extensive network of caves and karst formations. You can join guided cave exploration tours in places like the Wulong Karst Landscape to discover the region's underground wonders.

Before engaging in adventure sports in Chongqing, it's essential to consider safety measures, the expertise required, and any necessary permits or equipment. Many activities are seasonal, so be sure to check availability during your visit. Whether you're a seasoned adventurer or a beginner looking for an adrenaline rush, Chongqing's natural landscapes and outdoor opportunities have something to offer every level of thrill-seeker.

Chapter 11

DAY TRIPS AND NEARBY DESTINATIONS

Wulong Karst Landscape

Wulong Karst Landscape, a UNESCO World Heritage site, is a stunning natural destination located near Chongqing, which is known for its unique karst topography, deep canyons, and breathtaking landscapes. It's a fantastic place for a day trip from Chongqing, and it's renowned for its natural beauty and the backdrop for several famous films.

Here's what you can explore and experience during a day trip to the Wulong Karst Landscape:

1. **Three Natural Bridges (Tianlong Bridge, Qinglong Bridge, and Heilong Bridge):** These natural limestone bridges are the iconic features of Wulong. They span over deep canyons and provide incredible photo opportunities. You can hike

to viewpoints that offer breathtaking views of the bridges.

2. **Furong Cave (Furong Dong):** Furong Cave is a spectacular underground cave system with awe-inspiring stalactites and stalagmites. Guided tours are available to explore the cave's chambers and tunnels.

3. **Longshui Gorge (Longshuixia):** Longshui Gorge is famous for its crystal-clear waters and lush greenery. You can take a boat ride down the gorge, admiring the serene beauty of the karst landscape, including waterfalls and cliffs.

4. **Hiking and Nature Trails:** Wulong offers various hiking trails and nature walks that take you through the karst scenery and along pristine rivers. Some trails lead to secluded waterfalls and hidden caves.

5. **Zip-Lining:** For adventure enthusiasts, there are zip-line experiences available, allowing you to soar over the karst landscape for a thrilling view from above.

6. **Cultural Experiences:** In addition to natural attractions, you can learn about local culture and traditions. Don't miss the opportunity to explore traditional villages in the area.

7. **Movie Locations:** The Wulong Karst Landscape has been featured in several films, including "Transformers: Age of Extinction." You can visit film locations and reenact some of your favorite scenes.

8. **Picnicking:** There are designated areas where you can enjoy a picnic, making it a perfect spot to relax and savor the natural surroundings.

Wulong Karst Landscape is about a 2-3 hour drive from Chongqing, and it's a destination that offers a unique blend of natural wonders and cultural experiences. The karst terrain, lush forests, and serene waterways make it a place of breathtaking beauty. It's an ideal day trip for nature lovers, adventure seekers, and anyone looking to explore the captivating landscapes of southwestern China.

Fengdu Ghost City

Fengdu Ghost City is a unique cultural and historical site located about 170 kilometers (105 miles) from Chongqing. It's a popular day trip destination that provides visitors with a fascinating glimpse into Chinese folklore, beliefs, and the afterlife. Here's what you can expect when visiting Fengdu Ghost City:

1. **Ancient Mythology:** Fengdu Ghost City is steeped in ancient Chinese mythology related to the afterlife. It's believed to be a place where the spirits of the dead gather before moving on to the next realm. The city's architecture and sculptures are inspired by these legends.
2. **Scenic Overlooks:** The city is situated on Ming Mountain, and it offers stunning panoramic views of the Yangtze River and the surrounding landscape. There are several viewpoints that provide excellent photo opportunities.
3. **Ghostly Sculptures:** Fengdu Ghost City is known for its eerie and elaborate sculptures that depict various deities, mythical creatures, and historical figures from Chinese folklore. These sculptures can be both intriguing and slightly eerie.
4. **Numerous Temples and Shrines:** You'll find a range of temples and shrines within the city, each dedicated to different aspects of the afterlife. These temples are not only

architecturally fascinating but also culturally significant.

5. **Cultural Performances:** Fengdu Ghost City often hosts cultural performances and ceremonies that showcase traditional Chinese beliefs and practices related to death and the afterlife. These performances provide insight into the area's cultural heritage.

6. **Stairways and Paths:** The city is full of stairways, paths, and bridges that allow you to explore the area and its various temples. Walking through the city is an adventure in itself, with opportunities for discovery around every corner.

7. **Historical Significance:** Fengdu Ghost City has a long history dating back over 2,000 years. It has been associated with the Daoist and Confucian traditions, as well as ancient Chinese burial practices.

8. **Buddhist Influence:** While the city is primarily Daoist in nature, it also features elements of Buddhism, making it an intriguing blend of different religious and philosophical beliefs.

Fengdu Ghost City offers a unique cultural experience, and it's an excellent destination for those interested in history, mythology, and religious practices. The city is easily accessible from Chongqing and is a popular stop for visitors traveling along the Yangtze River or exploring the Three Gorges region. It provides a window into the rich and diverse cultural tapestry of China.

Ciqikou Ancient Town

Ciqikou Ancient Town, also known as "Porcelain Village," is a charming historic district located in the Shapingba District of Chongqing. It's a popular destination for both tourists and locals, offering a glimpse into traditional Chinese architecture, culture, and artisanal craftsmanship. Here's what you can expect when visiting Ciqikou Ancient Town:

1. **Ancient Architecture:** Ciqikou is known for its well-preserved traditional Chinese architecture. The town features narrow cobblestone streets, wooden buildings with upturned eaves, and intricate carvings. These architectural elements reflect the town's long history, dating back to the Ming and Qing dynasties.

2. **Local Crafts and Artisans:** Ciqikou is famous for its handicrafts, particularly porcelain and ceramics. As you wander through the town, you'll find numerous shops and workshops where artisans create and sell porcelain, tea sets, calligraphy, and other traditional Chinese crafts. You can often observe artisans at work, creating beautiful pieces of art.

3. **Teahouses and Snack Stalls:** The town is dotted with teahouses where you can relax and savor a cup of Chinese tea. Additionally, you can sample a variety of local snacks and street food, such as spicy Chongqing hotpot, stinky tofu, and sweet rice cakes.

4. **Historical Attractions:** Ciqikou Ancient Town is home to several historical sites and landmarks. You can explore the Buddhist temple of Baolun Si, the stilted house of Zhangfei Temple, and visit the Zhongtian Temple. These sites offer

insights into the town's cultural and religious heritage.

5. **Souvenir Shopping:** Ciqikou is an excellent place to shop for souvenirs and gifts. In addition to porcelain and ceramics, you'll find a wide range of traditional Chinese items, such as silk, handicrafts, artwork, and trinkets.

6. **Cultural Performances:** The town often hosts cultural performances, such as traditional music, puppet shows, and local opera, which provide a glimpse into the area's artistic and cultural heritage.

7. **Scenic Views:** Ciqikou is situated along the banks of the Jialing River, and you can enjoy picturesque views of the river and the surrounding hills. Many teahouses and cafes have outdoor seating, allowing you to relax while taking in the scenery.

8. **Festivals and Events:** Ciqikou hosts various festivals and events throughout the year, with special celebrations during traditional Chinese holidays and cultural festivals.

Ciqikou Ancient Town is a popular day trip destination from Chongqing, offering a delightful blend of history, culture, and craftsmanship. It's an excellent place to immerse yourself in traditional Chinese heritage, savor local cuisine, and explore the town's unique character. The town's relaxed ambiance and scenic surroundings make it a favorite spot for visitors seeking an authentic cultural experience.

Other Nearby Attractions

Chongqing and its surrounding areas are rich in attractions and natural beauty. If you have more time to explore the region, here are some other nearby attractions worth considering for day trips or extended visits:

1. **Three Gorges Dam:** Located in Yichang, Hubei Province, the Three Gorges Dam is one of the world's largest hydropower projects. You can take a cruise to visit the dam and learn about its significance in managing the Yangtze River.

2. **Dazu Rock Carvings:** The Dazu Rock Carvings, a UNESCO World Heritage site, are located in Dazu County, Chongqing. These ancient rock carvings feature Buddhist, Taoist, and Confucian sculptures and inscriptions carved into the cliffs.

3. **Chongqing Hot Springs:** Chongqing is known for its natural hot springs, and there are several hot spring resorts in the area. A day trip or weekend getaway to a hot spring resort is a relaxing experience.

4. **Wansheng Black Valley Scenic Area:** Located in Wansheng District, Chongqing, this scenic area offers adventures like bungee jumping, rock climbing, and hiking, as well as opportunities to enjoy natural beauty.

5. **Jiulong Waterfall Scenic Area:** Jiulong Waterfall, located in Youyang County, Chongqing, is known for its stunning cascades and lush forests. It's an ideal destination for nature lovers and hikers.

6. **Wulong Tiansheng Three Bridges:** In addition to the famous natural bridges, Wulong also features other karst formations and attractions like Houping Tiankeng (sink-

hole) and Qingkou Tiankeng.

7. **Furong Cave:** Furong Cave, located in Wulong County, is one of China's most famous karst caves. It features impressive stalactites, stalagmites, and underground chambers.

8. **Chongqing Wuling Mountain National Park:** Situated in the northern suburbs of Chongqing, this national park offers hiking, picturesque landscapes, and a chance to explore the natural beauty of the Wuling Mountains.

9. **Dianjiang Thousand Island Lake:** Dianjiang County is home to the Thousand Island Lake, a picturesque reservoir surrounded by green hills and clear waters. You can take boat tours or enjoy water sports.

10. **Fuling Shibanpo Yangtze River Bridge and Tieshanping Forest Park:** Fuling is known for its cable-stayed bridge over the Yangtze River and the nearby Tieshanping Forest Park, which offers hiking trails and scenic viewpoints.

11. **Wuxiandong Karst Cave:** Located in Wulong County, this cave features impressive karst formations, an underground river, and colorful lighting that creates a mesmerizing visual experience.

Each of these attractions offers a unique experience, whether you're interested in history, nature, adventure, or cultural exploration. Depending on your interests and the time you have available, you can plan day trips or longer excursions to explore the diverse attractions surrounding Chongqing.

Chapter 12

PRACTICAL INFORMATION

Visa and Entry Requirements

T o visit Chongqing, China, and its surrounding areas, you will typically need to obtain a Chinese visa unless you are eligible for visa-free entry or transit without a visa. Here are some key points to consider regarding visa and entry requirements:

1. **Visa Categories:**

- Tourist Visa (L Visa): This is the most common visa type for leisure travel to Chongqing. It's typically issued for tourism, family visits, or other non-business purposes.

1. **Visa-Free Entry:**

· Some nationalities are eligible for visa-free entry to Chongqing and other parts of China for a limited period, depending on bilateral agreements. However, the duration of stay and eligibility can vary, so it's crucial to check with the nearest Chinese embassy or consulate for the most up-to-date information.

1. **Transit Without Visa (TWOV):**

· Chongqing Jiangbei International Airport may offer the 24-hour or 72-hour Transit Without Visa (TWOV) option for passengers in transit. This allows you to stay in Chongqing for a specific period without a visa if you are transiting to a third country. Eligibility and conditions apply, and you should check with the airport authorities for the latest information.

1. **Visa Application:**

· To obtain a Chinese tourist visa, you typically need to apply at the nearest Chinese embassy or consulate in your home country or country of residence. The required documents often include a completed visa application form, a valid passport with at least six months of validity, a passport-sized photo, proof of accommodation reservations, round-trip flight tickets, and a detailed travel itinerary.

1. **Visa Duration and Entries:**

· Chinese tourist visas can be issued as single-entry, double-entry, or multiple-entry visas, with varying durations.

Ensure you choose the appropriate type and duration based on your travel plans.

1. **Visa Extension:**

· If you wish to extend your stay in China while in Chongqing, you may apply for a visa extension at the local Public Security Bureau's Exit and Entry Administration office. Be sure to apply for an extension before your current visa expires.

1. **Visa Regulations and Entry Points:**

· Chongqing has several entry points, including Chongqing Jiangbei International Airport and land border crossings with neighboring countries. Ensure that you enter China through a designated port of entry for your visa type.

1. **Health and Travel Insurance:**

· It's advisable to have travel insurance that includes coverage for medical emergencies, as well as trip cancellation and other contingencies.

1. **Local Registration:**

· Upon arrival in China, you should register your accommodation with the local police within 24 hours of arrival. Most hotels will assist you with this registration, but be sure to inquire at check-in.

1. **Local Customs and Laws:**

· Familiarize yourself with local customs and laws in Chongqing and China. Respect cultural norms, and be aware of any specific rules or regulations that may apply to tourists.

Always check with the nearest Chinese embassy or consulate for the most current and specific visa requirements and application procedures based on your nationality and individual circumstances. Additionally, it's recommended to begin the visa application process well in advance of your planned travel dates to allow for processing time.

Currency and Banking

When traveling to Chongqing, China, it's essential to be aware of the local currency and banking practices to manage your finances efficiently. Here's some practical information about currency and banking in Chongqing:

1. **Currency:** The official currency of China is the Renminbi (RMB), and the basic unit of currency is the Yuan (CNY).
2. **Banknotes and Coins:** Common banknotes in circulation are ¥1, ¥5, ¥10, ¥20, ¥50, and ¥100. There are also smaller denominations and coins, although coins are not widely used in everyday transactions.
3. **Currency Exchange:** Currency exchange services are available at Chongqing Jiangbei International Airport, local banks, and authorized exchange counters in tourist areas. Major foreign currencies such as US dollars and euros can

be exchanged easily. It's advisable to keep some Chinese currency on hand for small purchases and transportation.

4. **ATMs:** ATMs (Automatic Teller Machines) are widespread in Chongqing, and most accept international debit and credit cards such as Visa, MasterCard, and UnionPay. Look for ATMs affiliated with major banks like Bank of China, Industrial and Commercial Bank of China (ICBC), and China Construction Bank. Ensure your bank card has been enabled for international use before traveling.

5. **Credit Cards:** Credit cards are accepted at many hotels, upscale restaurants, and larger stores in Chongqing. Major credit cards like Visa and MasterCard are more widely accepted than others. However, be prepared to use cash for smaller, local businesses, street vendors, and public transportation.

6. **Mobile Payments:** Mobile payment systems like Alipay and WeChat Pay are popular in China. These digital wallets can be linked to your bank card and are commonly used for transactions at various businesses. To use mobile payments, you'll need to download the respective app and link it to your bank card or deposit cash into your digital wallet.

7. **Banks and Banking Hours:** Major Chinese banks operate in Chongqing, and they typically provide currency exchange services, ATMs, and assistance for foreign visitors. Banking hours are generally from 9:00 AM to 5:00 PM, Monday to Friday. Some banks may have limited Saturday hours.

8. **Traveler's Cheques:** Traveler's cheques are not as widely accepted as they once were, and it can be challenging to find places to cash them. It's recommended to rely on a combination of cash, credit/debit cards, and mobile

payments for your financial needs.

9. **Safety:** Be cautious when using ATMs, and try to use machines located in well-lit, secure areas. It's wise to shield your PIN while entering it, and be aware of your surroundings when making transactions.

10. **Foreign Exchange Record:** If you exchange more than ¥5,000 or its equivalent in foreign currency, keep the exchange receipt. This record may be required when converting your unused RMB back to foreign currency before departing China.

Before traveling, inform your bank about your international travel plans to avoid card issues due to security measures. Additionally, carry a small amount of Chinese currency in case you encounter businesses that do not accept cards or digital payments. By being prepared and informed about currency and banking in Chongqing, you'll have a smoother and more convenient experience managing your finances during your visit.

Internet and Communication

Staying connected to the internet and having reliable communication methods while in Chongqing is essential for travelers. Here's what you need to know about internet access and communication options in the city:

Internet Access:

1. **Wi-Fi:** Many hotels, restaurants, cafes, and public spaces in Chongqing offer free Wi-Fi for customers. Look for signs indicating "Free Wi-Fi" or "Wi-Fi" (public Wi-Fi).
2. **Mobile Data:** To have continuous internet access, consider purchasing a local SIM card with a data plan. China Mobile, China Unicom, and China Telecom are the major mobile service providers in China. You can buy SIM cards at the airport, convenience stores, or official stores of these providers. Ensure your phone is unlocked and compatible with Chinese networks.
3. **Pocket Wi-Fi (Mobile Hotspot):** You can rent a portable Wi-Fi device, often referred to as a pocket Wi-Fi or mobile hotspot, which provides a stable internet connection for multiple devices. These devices can be rented at the airport, online, or from certain providers in the city.

Communication:

1. **Local Phone Calls:** If you need to make local phone calls within China, you can purchase a local SIM card. Make sure your phone is unlocked for compatibility.
2. **International Calls:** International phone calls can be made from your hotel, public phone booths, or through international calling cards. Dial the international access code (00), the country code, and then the phone number.
3. **Messaging Apps:** Popular messaging apps like WeChat, WhatsApp, and Telegram work well in China and are used for text and voice communication. WeChat, in particular, is widely used for various purposes, including communication, mobile payments, and social networking.

4. **Emergency Numbers:** In case of an emergency, dial 110 for police, 120 for medical assistance, and 119 for fire services. These numbers are toll-free and should be dialed directly from your phone.

5. **Language Barrier:** While English is spoken at major tourist locations, many locals may not be fluent. Having translation apps, phrasebooks, or basic Mandarin phrases can be helpful for communication.

6. **VPN (Virtual Private Network):** Access to some international websites and social media platforms may be restricted in China due to the Great Firewall. To bypass these restrictions, you can use a VPN service. Before traveling, download and install a VPN app on your device.

Remember that communication and internet access may vary depending on your location within Chongqing. In urban areas and popular tourist spots, you are more likely to have reliable connectivity. Be sure to prepare for your communication and internet needs before your trip to Chongqing to ensure a smooth and enjoyable experience.

Health and Safety

Ensuring your health and safety while visiting Chongqing is of paramount importance. Here are some key considerations and tips for staying healthy and safe during your trip:

Health:

1. **Vaccinations:** Check with your healthcare provider to ensure you are up-to-date on routine vaccinations and inquire about any recommended vaccinations for travel to China.

2. **Food and Water Safety:** Be cautious about the food and water you consume. Stick to bottled water for drinking, and avoid consuming raw or undercooked food. Chongqing is famous for its spicy hotpot, but make sure the ingredients are thoroughly cooked.

3. **Prescription Medications:** If you require prescription medications, bring an ample supply for your entire trip. Carry a copy of your prescription and the generic name of the medication in case you need a refill.

4. **Travel Insurance:** Consider purchasing comprehensive travel insurance that covers medical emergencies and evacuation. Verify what is covered in your policy and carry relevant contact information.

5. **Pharmacies:** Chongqing has numerous pharmacies, and you can find both Western and traditional Chinese medicines. However, it's helpful to have your medications labeled in Chinese or to know the generic names.

6. **Air Quality:** Check the air quality index before engaging in outdoor activities, as Chongqing can experience periods of air pollution, especially in the winter. Wearing a mask can help protect against air pollution.

7. **Mosquito Protection:** If you plan to explore outdoor areas or visit during the summer months, consider using mosquito repellent to protect against mosquito-borne diseases.

Safety:

1. **Travel Advisories:** Stay updated on travel advisories issued by your country's embassy or consulate in China. Familiarize yourself with local laws and customs.

2. **Scams:** Be cautious of common travel scams, including overcharging in taxis, counterfeit currency, and unauthorized tour operators. Always use registered taxis, and ask for a metered fare.

3. **Local Laws:** Abide by Chinese laws and regulations. For instance, it's illegal to use VPNs to access blocked websites. Also, avoid discussing sensitive topics, such as politics or religion.

4. **Traffic Safety:** Exercise caution when crossing streets, as traffic can be chaotic. Use marked pedestrian crossings, and be aware that traffic may not always yield to pedestrians.

5. **Emergency Services:** Save important contact information, such as the local embassy or consulate, your country's embassy, local police (110), and medical services (120), in your phone.

6. **Language Barrier:** Expect some language barriers, as English may not be widely spoken outside major tourist areas. Carry a translation app or a phrasebook to help with communication.

7. **Crowded Places:** Be vigilant in crowded areas to protect your belongings. Consider using anti-theft bags or pouches to safeguard your valuables.

8. **Night Safety:** While Chongqing is generally safe, exercise caution when out at night, especially in less crowded areas. Stay in well-lit, populated areas.

9. **Natural Hazards:** Pay attention to local weather and any natural hazards like floods, landslides, or earthquakes. Be

prepared for changes in weather and follow local advice.

10. **Travel Itinerary:** Share your travel itinerary with someone you trust. Let them know where you plan to go and when you expect to return.

Remember that safety and health concerns can vary based on your specific activities and the time of year you visit. Staying informed and taking precautions are key to ensuring a safe and enjoyable trip to Chongqing.

Packing Tips

Packing for your trip to Chongqing requires consideration of the city's climate and cultural norms. Here are some packing tips to help you prepare for your visit:

Clothing:

1. **Light and Breathable Clothes:** Chongqing has a humid sub-tropical climate, so pack lightweight, breathable clothing suitable for warm and humid conditions. Cotton and linen materials are good choices.
2. **Rain Gear:** Chongqing can experience heavy rain, especially during the summer. An umbrella or a lightweight, packable rain jacket is a wise addition to your luggage.
3. **Comfortable Shoes:** Bring comfortable walking shoes for exploring the city and its hilly terrain. If you plan to visit outdoor attractions, consider closed-toe shoes suitable for hiking or walking on uneven terrain.

4. **Layers:** Evenings can be cooler, so pack a light jacket or sweater for cooler nights. Additionally, pack a swimsuit if you plan to visit hot springs or water parks.
5. **Modest Clothing:** When visiting religious sites or traditional villages, dress modestly to show respect. For women, it's a good idea to have a scarf or shawl to cover your shoulders if needed.

Travel Essentials:

1. **Travel Adapters:** China uses Type A and Type I electrical outlets. Depending on your home country, you may need a plug adapter and a voltage converter.
2. **Portable Charger:** Ensure your devices stay charged while you're out and about. A portable charger can be a lifesaver.
3. **Travel Documents:** Carry essential travel documents, including your passport, visa, travel insurance, and printed copies of hotel reservations and travel itineraries.
4. **Prescription Medications:** Bring an adequate supply of any prescription medications you'll need during your trip.
5. **Language Aid:** Pack a phrasebook or translation app to help with communication, as English may not be widely spoken in some areas.
6. **Cash and Cards:** Have a mix of cash (in local currency) and cards. Notify your bank of your travel plans to prevent any card issues.

Travel Gear:

1. **Backpack:** A small backpack is useful for day trips and carrying essentials while exploring the city.
2. **Anti-Theft Gear:** Consider using anti-theft bags, pouches, or wallets to protect your belongings from pickpockets.
3. **Travel Pillow and Eye Mask:** These can be handy for long flights or train journeys and for getting rest during your travels.
4. **Reusable Water Bottle:** Staying hydrated is crucial, so having a reusable water bottle can save you money and reduce plastic waste.

Toiletries and Health:

1. **Basic Toiletries:** Pack personal hygiene items, including travel-sized shampoo, soap, toothbrush, and toothpaste.
2. **Prescription Glasses and Medications:** If you wear glasses or take medications, ensure you have them on hand.
3. **Sunscreen and Bug Repellent:** Protect your skin from the sun and potential insects, especially if you plan to explore outdoor areas.
4. **First-Aid Kit:** Bring a basic first-aid kit with essentials like band-aids, antiseptic wipes, pain relievers, and any necessary medications.

Cultural Considerations:

1. **Modest Dress:** As previously mentioned, be mindful of the local culture when visiting temples or traditional villages. Carry appropriate clothing.

2. **Gifts and Souvenirs:** If you plan to exchange gifts or souvenirs with locals, consider small, non-perishable items from your home country.

Remember to check the weather forecast for Chongqing before packing, as conditions can vary depending on the time of year. By preparing well and packing appropriately, you'll be ready for a comfortable and enjoyable visit to Chongqing.

Chapter 13

PLANNING YOUR ITINERARY

Sample Itineraries

C reating a sample itinerary for your visit to Chongqing can help you make the most of your time in this vibrant city. Chongqing offers a mix of cultural attractions, natural beauty, and delicious cuisine. Here are two sample itineraries to choose from, depending on your interests and the duration of your stay:

Sample Itinerary 1: Chongqing Highlights (3 Days)
Day 1: Arrival in Chongqing

- Morning:
- Arrive at Chongqing Jiangbei International Airport.
- Check in to your hotel in the downtown area.
- Afternoon:

- Visit Ciqikou Ancient Town, stroll through its historic streets, and explore local shops.
- Enjoy a Sichuan hotpot dinner at a local restaurant.

Day 2: Exploring the City

- Morning:
- Have breakfast at your hotel or a local eatery.
- Explore Eling Park, known for its gardens, viewpoints, and cultural significance.
- Visit Chongqing Zoo and Aquarium to see a variety of animals and marine life.
- Afternoon:
- Head to the Three Gorges Museum to learn about the region's history and culture.
- Explore the Jiefangbei shopping district and enjoy some shopping.
- Evening:
- Dine at a local restaurant in Jiefangbei or try a riverside eatery along the Yangtze River.

Day 3: Natural Beauty and Departure

- Morning:
- Drive to the Wulong Karst Landscape for a day trip. Explore the natural bridges and caves.
- Have a picnic lunch in the scenic area.
- Afternoon:
- Return to Chongqing and relax at your hotel.
- Visit Hongyadong for picturesque views of the city and enjoy a meal at one of the restaurants.

- Evening:
- Depart from Chongqing, either by flight or other means.

Sample Itinerary 2: Extended Exploration (5 Days)

Day 1: Arrival and Cultural Experiences

- Arrive in Chongqing and check in to your hotel.
- Explore Ciqikou Ancient Town, its local crafts, and enjoy a traditional Sichuan dinner.

Day 2: Chongqing's Top Attractions

- Visit Eling Park, Chongqing Zoo, and the Three Gorges Museum.
- Explore Chongqing's shopping districts, including Jiefang-bei.

Day 3: Day Trip to Fengdu Ghost City

- Take a day trip to Fengdu Ghost City, exploring the unique cultural and historical site.
- Return to Chongqing in the evening.

Day 4: Nature and Karst Landscape

- Drive to the Wulong Karst Landscape for a full day of exploration.
- Enjoy the natural bridges, caves, and scenic beauty.

Day 5: Culinary Adventures and Departure

- Visit Hongyadong for picturesque views and enjoy local cuisine.
- Depart from Chongqing with wonderful memories.

These itineraries are designed to provide you with a taste of Chongqing's diverse offerings, from cultural experiences to natural beauty and culinary delights. You can adjust the itineraries based on your interests, the time available, and the season of your visit. Chongqing has much to offer, and you'll find something to suit your preferences, whether you're interested in history, nature, or gastronomy.

- Travel Tips for Different Seasons

Chongqing experiences distinct seasons, and the best travel tips can vary depending on when you plan to visit. Here are travel tips for each season to help you make the most of your trip:

Spring (March to May):

1. **Weather:** Spring in Chongqing is generally pleasant, with mild temperatures and occasional rain. Bring layers and a light jacket for cooler evenings.
2. **Scenic Tours:** Spring is an excellent time to explore Chongqing's natural beauty. Visit parks and gardens, such as Eling Park and the Chongqing Botanical Garden, to see cherry blossoms and various flowers in bloom.
3. **Outdoor Activities:** Plan outdoor excursions to Wulong

Karst Landscape and other natural attractions. The weather is comfortable for hiking and sightseeing.

Summer (June to August):

1. **Weather:** Chongqing's summer is hot and humid, with occasional heavy rain showers. Dress in lightweight, breathable clothing and carry an umbrella or rain jacket.
2. **Stay Hydrated:** The heat can be intense, so drink plenty of water and stay hydrated. Avoid overexertion, especially during the hottest part of the day.
3. **Chongqing Hotpot:** Try Chongqing's famous hotpot, but be prepared for the spice! It's a great way to experience local cuisine.
4. **Indoor Attractions:** Visit museums, shopping districts, and indoor attractions during the hottest part of the day to escape the sun.

Autumn (September to November):

1. **Weather:** Autumn is one of the best times to visit Chongqing. The weather is pleasant with cooler temperatures and less rainfall. Bring light layers for varying temperatures.
2. **Cultural Events:** Check for local festivals and events that may be happening during your visit. Autumn is a great time to witness cultural celebrations.
3. **Fall Foliage:** If visiting in late autumn, explore parks and natural areas to see the beautiful fall foliage.

Winter (December to February):

1. **Weather:** Chongqing's winter is mild compared to other parts of China, but it can still get cold, especially in the evenings. Bring warm clothing, including a coat and layers.
2. **Hot Springs:** Chongqing is known for its hot springs. Consider a visit to one of the local hot spring resorts to warm up and relax.
3. **Indoor Attractions:** Spend time exploring indoor attractions, such as museums and shopping malls. This is also an excellent time for culinary adventures.
4. **Chinese New Year:** If your visit coincides with Chinese New Year (dates vary), experience the festive atmosphere, traditional performances, and local customs.

General Tips for All Seasons:

1. **Book Accommodation in Advance:** Chongqing is a popular destination, so book your accommodation in advance, especially during peak travel seasons.
2. **Public Transportation:** Familiarize yourself with Chongqing's public transportation system, including the metro and buses. It's an efficient way to get around the city.
3. **Local Cuisine:** Don't miss out on trying the local cuisine, including Chongqing hotpot, but be mindful of the spice level if you're not used to it.
4. **Language:** While some locals may speak English, it's helpful to have basic Mandarin phrases or a translation app to assist with communication.
5. **Travel Insurance:** Consider purchasing travel insurance to

cover unexpected events or emergencies during your trip.

Chongqing offers something unique in every season, so choose the time that aligns with your preferences, and be prepared for the weather and activities accordingly. Whether you're exploring natural wonders, enjoying cultural events, or savoring local dishes, Chongqing has a lot to offer year-round.

Traveling with Children

Traveling with children to Chongqing can be a fun and rewarding experience, but it also requires some extra planning and consideration. Here are some tips to help ensure a smooth and enjoyable family trip to Chongqing:

1. Travel Documents:

- Ensure that each family member, including children, has valid passports and any required visas.
- Make copies of important travel documents, such as passports and visas, and keep them separate from the originals.

2. Health and Safety:

- Research any required vaccinations or health precautions for traveling to Chongqing with children. Check with your healthcare provider before your trip.
- Pack a basic first-aid kit that includes items like band-aids, antiseptic wipes, and over-the-counter medications suitable for children.

3. Accommodation:

- Choose family-friendly accommodations with amenities like cribs, rollaway beds, and adjoining rooms if needed.
- Inquire with your hotel or accommodation about childproofing options if you have younger children.

4. Child Carriers:

- If you plan to explore natural attractions, consider bringing a comfortable child carrier or stroller for younger children.

5. Packing Essentials:

- Pack essential items for children, including diapers, baby wipes, baby food, and any special formula or food they require.
- Bring entertainment for children, such as toys, coloring books, and tablets with games or educational apps for long flights or waiting times.

6. Safety Gear:

- Chongqing's traffic can be chaotic, so consider bringing child safety seats for any transportation, including taxis.
- Teach your children basic safety rules, such as looking both ways before crossing streets, and keeping a safe distance from traffic.

7. Accommodate Food Preferences:

- Chongqing's cuisine can be spicy, so make sure there are suitable food options for children. Many restaurants offer mild or non-spicy dishes.

8. Learn Basic Phrases:

- While English may not be widely spoken, learning some basic Mandarin phrases can be helpful. Teach children a few essential phrases like "hello" and "thank you."

9. Child Identification:

- Ensure your children have identification on them, such as a laminated card with their name and your contact information in both English and Chinese.

10. Plan Kid-Friendly Activities:

- Research child-friendly attractions in Chongqing, such as the Chongqing Zoo, children's museums, and parks.
- Check for special events or festivals that may be of interest to children during your visit.

11. Transportation:

- Use child-friendly transportation options, such as metro and buses, which are generally safe and convenient for families.

12. Safety Precautions:

- Be vigilant in crowded areas to ensure the safety of your children and protect your belongings.
- Have a meeting point in case you get separated from your child in a crowded place.

13. Local Assistance:

- Seek assistance from locals or other travelers if you need directions or help with translation.

Traveling with children in Chongqing can be an enriching experience, allowing them to discover a different culture and create lasting memories. Proper preparation, safety measures, and flexibility will help ensure a positive family travel experience in this vibrant city.

Solo Travel

Traveling solo to Chongqing can be a rewarding and exciting experience. Here are some tips to make the most of your solo adventure in this vibrant city:

1. Research and Planning:

- Start by thoroughly researching Chongqing, its attractions, and the best times to visit.
- Plan your itinerary and make a list of the places you want to explore.

2. Accommodation:

- Choose accommodation in safe and convenient areas of the city, such as the downtown district or near public transportation.
- Consider staying in hostels or guesthouses, which can be excellent places to meet fellow travelers and locals.

3. Language:

- While English is not widely spoken, learning a few basic Mandarin phrases can go a long way in helping you communicate and connect with locals.

4. Safety:

- Chongqing is generally a safe city, but like any destination, exercise common-sense safety precautions. Keep your belongings secure, especially in crowded areas.
- Let someone know your travel plans and itinerary, and check in with them regularly.

5. Transportation:

- Chongqing has an efficient public transportation system, including buses and a metro. Familiarize yourself with the routes and schedules to get around the city easily.

6. Local Cuisine:

- Chongqing is known for its spicy Sichuan cuisine, including the famous Chongqing hotpot. Don't miss the chance to savor local dishes, but be prepared for the spice.

- Try street food and local markets for authentic culinary experiences.

7. Socialize:

- Consider joining group tours, meetups, or language exchange events to meet fellow travelers or locals.
- Hostels often organize group activities and social events that are great for solo travelers.

8. Local Culture:

- Immerse yourself in local culture by attending cultural events, visiting traditional markets, and exploring local neighborhoods.

9. Stay Connected:

- Ensure you have a working phone with a local SIM card or an international roaming plan to stay connected.
- Download travel apps, including maps, translation, and transportation apps, to make your journey easier.

10. Flexibility:

- Embrace spontaneity. Sometimes the best experiences are the ones you didn't plan for.
- Be open to changing your itinerary based on recommendations from fellow travelers or locals.

11. Solo Enjoyment:

- Solo travel is an opportunity for self-discovery. Enjoy the freedom to do what you want when you want, without the need for compromise.

12. Safety at Night:

- While Chongqing is generally safe at night, be cautious in less crowded areas and choose well-lit routes. Avoid overindulgence and stay aware of your surroundings.

13. Learn About Local Customs:

- Familiarize yourself with local customs and etiquette. For example, it's polite to accept and offer gifts with both hands and to show respect in temples and traditional villages.

Solo travel in Chongqing can provide you with a unique perspective on this dynamic city. With proper planning and an adventurous spirit, you'll have the chance to create lasting memories and gain a deeper understanding of Chongqing's rich culture and history.

14

Conclusion

I n conclusion, "Chongqing Travel Guide" offers a comprehensive journey through the heart of this remarkable city, providing readers with invaluable insights, practical advice, and a deep understanding of the culture, history, and attractions that make Chongqing a captivating destination.

From the bustling streets of Jiefangbei to the tranquil beauty of Eling Park, from the fiery flavors of Chongqing hotpot to the rich history of the Three Gorges Dam, this guide has taken you on a memorable exploration of the city's diverse offerings. Whether you're a solo adventurer seeking self-discovery, a family eager for shared experiences, or a traveler with a penchant for culinary delights and natural wonders, Chongqing has something to offer you.

As you prepare for your journey to Chongqing, remember to embrace the unique blend of tradition and modernity, immerse yourself in the rich culture and warm hospitality of its people, and savor every moment in this incredible destination.

Chongqing is a city that leaves an indelible mark on all who visit, and with the knowledge and tips from this guide, you are well-equipped to embark on an unforgettable adventure.

May your travels in Chongqing be filled with wonder, new connections, and cherished memories, as you discover the heart and soul of this dynamic city. Safe travels, and may Chongqing's beauty and spirit captivate you, just as it has captivated countless visitors before you.

Printed in Great Britain
by Amazon

36947408R00106